Field Tips

Retail Business Improvement Writings

David W. McMahon, CMA

ISBN: 1479194522
ISBN-13: **978-1479194520**

DEDICATION

Raja, Chase, Vela

WRITINGS

WRITINGS

WRITINGS

WRITINGS

ACKNOWLEDGMENTS

I would like to thank my father and business partner Wayne McMahon. It has been a fun ride so far. I'd also like to thank Russell Bienenstock, the CEO at Furniture World, the team at PROFIT*systems* Inc., the NHFA and WHFA for publishing my articles in their journals and newsletters. Many thanks to PROFITsystems for finding creative solutions to help retailers solve their problems. During my many years of working with the great people there I have learned and grown in my understanding of business, and feel privileged to be able to pass some of the insights on to others. Finally, thank you to all the businesses and people to whom I have consulted with, around the world.

INTRO

Field Tips is an updated compilation of my best practice writings. It based on my observations as an in-the-field Business Consultant primarily in Retail. Since 1999 I have travelled the world helping people improve themselves and their teams. I have gained tremendous insight from my experiences and wish to share my knowledge with you.

I have been exposed to the best of the best, the worst of the worst, and everything in between. The overriding thing that I learned is that anyone can improve with the right attitude, belief, commitment and education.

Field Tips is laid out into 3 sections: Operations, Inventory, and Financial. It is also in a blog-like format. That means that you can read from start to finish or just go to whatever writing looks interesting depending on your mood or current business challenge.

My hope is that you are both entertained and educated. Take some of the gems from this book, tweak them, and make them your own. You will improve your business.

Enjoy!

David

Operations

1. WHAT ARE YOU SEEING OUT THERE?

This is one of the most common questions I get. Business people want to know: "What is happening in other businesses around the retail world? How are they doing in this economy? How are consumers responding? What is working? What is not working? Are consumers buying? Is the general economic feeling up or down?"

Here is what my experiences are telling me:

There is no doubt that we went through the worst recession in America since the great depression. It was the biggest that I have experienced in America in my career. The primary U.S. stock market (Dow Jones Industrial Average) fell from a high of 14,500 to a low of 6,500. Trillions of dollars evaporated. Along with this, unemployment rose steadily as consumer spending plummeted.

Independent retailers sure felt their fair share of this loss. We can all name numerous companies that have gone out of business in the past few years. For those companies that hung on, I've seen some with 50% drops in sales from their "glory days." 20% declines were commonplace.

That said, there were bright spots. Select operations busted their butts, worked smarter, and innovated to avoid the crippling declines of their competitors.

The smart operations realized that there was something as important as sales: PROFITABILITY!

Profits are a prerequisite and determinant of sales growth. With the recession, I saw that the most profitable companies before were still the most profitable companies during, and are now the most profitable companies after. This was independent of what happened to their customer traffic and their sales.

Great businesses strive to remain the same great businesses whether in recession or boom.

In my opinion, great businesses are defined as organizations with people that embrace learning, innovation, efficiency, self-investment, integrity, and respect for all. They mandate excellence and high profitability. They can make quick decisions, manage professionally, and execute their strategies. They enjoy the process of getting better at what they do.

So, what's next?

The recession of the 1st decade of the 3rd millennium ran its course. The stock market came back up. The economy and retail sales have stabilized and increased in certain sectors. Revenues stopped declining nationwide.

It is time to forget the past – now is the new normal.

Smart companies restructured themselves during the downturn. Many business that I am working with now are seeing all time record dollar profit levels even though their sales levels are not at record levels in many cases.

Businesses are becoming efficient at their new sales normal. They are maintaining a proper inventory mix, capturing appropriate gross margin, changing marketing methods, and investing in expenses that add to rather than take away from their operations.

I can't overemphasize that it is extremely important that you have decent profitability when your economy is in recovery mode.

Your level of profitability will determine whether you will outlast your competition that may not be as efficient. Greater efficiency allows you to reap maximum benefits with any upticks in customer traffic produced by economic growth. It allows you to minimize impacts of sudden downturns, as well.

If you are not maximizing your profitability now, seek to do so quickly.

Don't worry about the PAST. It is not that important. It does not matter if sales once were double where they are now. What matters is NOW!!! Get your business in order NOW. Build your productivity and profitability NOW. NOW is the new normal. Your future will thank you.

2. THE FAMILY FACTOR

Many of you reading this are either in business with family members or working for a business with family members in management. This is the nature of small to mid-sized business in America. Even the largest retailers in the world like Wal-Mart and Ikea are "family-born" companies.

Depending on the strength and quality of this family factor, some businesses see success and riches while others give way to failure and bankruptcy.

It can be a huge advantage in doing business, if the family members work well together. I have seen great achievements where all members communicate openly and have clear job functions that they execute with professionalism.

I have also seen good companies that have been in business for many years, become ruined, because the generation that assumed control was not properly educated in managing in today's workplace. Legacy issues also arise when older generations refuse to pass the baton and step aside.

Independent operations that fail to reach their potential often have family management who are paid as well as hired professionals, but do not perform like professionals.

However, if the family members are professionals and out-perform your competition's team, you will set the stage to produce greater results. Hold yourself to the highest standards!

Members who complement and respect each other in the workplace, prosper together. This is not just a natural occurrence. High profit family businesses take various actions to continually improve themselves including:

- They communicate as professionals with respect.

- Have formal job descriptions outlining duties and expectations.

- Meet the job requirements.

- Set goals and targets for which they are measured.

- Use pay for performance compensation plans.

- Attend regular operations and management meetings.

- Attend industry seminars and use performance groups.

- Are evaluated by others.

- Are truly qualified in their position.

- Improve themselves though continual professional training.

- Are up to date and are using the latest technology. They are innovators.

- Help others improve and develop.

Competency and commitment of all business members help determine success. For example, if one member is a buyer, she needs to be competent in inventory management. If another member is an office manager, he should be responsible for producing on time and accurate monthly financial reports and analysis for management. If you have a CFO that is a family member, she should possess the proper background. And if another is a sales manager, he should be capable of setting and monitoring sales targets, tracking metrics, and developing salespeople.

I know firsthand that working in a family based business can be hugely rewarding and loads of fun. I have been involved in several over the past 25 years and have seen huge successes in this fantastic business model, when done right.

3. CHAIN OF OPERATIONS

All business models function in a chain of activities. Each job function or process is a link in a chain playing a critical role in adding value to the previous function. It, in turn, passes on value to the next function. If there is a weak link (or constraint) in your chain of operations, it will eventually break, causing operational bottlenecks. Ultimately, that results in lower sales and profits due to a less than optimal customer experience.

Let's use the purchase process as an example. Suppose a customer wishes to special-order a table in a department store. She reviews all the details with her salesperson who writes up a sales order. The sales order is given to the purchasing manager who keys in the PO and specifies a flat black finish. The merchandise arrives, the delivery is scheduled and then the product is delivered. When the customer sees her table, she is dismayed. She wanted a glossy black finish and asks for a refund.

This is just one example of hundreds of breaks that occur in the chain of operations. If this business had a stronger link between the salesperson and the purchasing process, this kind of problem could have been avoided.

The diagram following represents various links in the chain of a retail operation. Each role must be completed perfectly before proceeding to the next link in the chain.

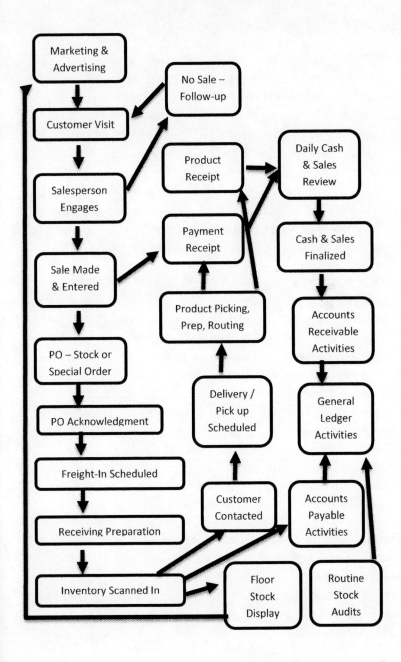

Critical Links in the Chain of Operations

Marketing: The first link in your business chain is obvious. It is the role of marketing. There is no business without customers. Whatever your media and networking combination, its purpose is to obtain relevant sales leads. If your product is high-end luxury contemporary merchandise for example, you probably don't want high school kids visiting you. You would much prefer a high income, style conscious customer, right? So, that's where your marketing focus should be. Know your customer and target your efforts directly to that audience. Businesses with a strong first link will get more selling opportunities. Businesses with a broken first link don't produce enough leads and have a difficult time growing their operations.

Initial Customer Visit & Salesperson Engagement: Serving your customer professionally is the goal of engagement. This is where a good CRM (customer relations management) system can help. Salespeople work with customers to help them discover and solve purchasing challenges. A certain percentage of customers do not buy on their initial visit, however. That's why capturing customer visit data is so important. This can be done through a variety of methods ranging from traffic counters, to VIP draws to writing up quotes. The next best thing to a buying customer is one who leaves after giving you their contact information. Which leads to the next link...

Follow Up with CRM: The only purpose of a lead is to follow up on it. If there is no system to follow-up on leads, most will die a quick death. CRM encourages this follow-up. Customers who give you their information deserve to be contacted. To increase your chance of getting through, contact them with a relevant communication in a media that they prefer. If they signed up for your VIP list, send them a monthly email with a discount or drawing opportunity. If they got a quote, call and email them a product update with information to help them make their decision.

You will find that top salespeople have a talent for follow-up. Use a

CRM system to help your average salespeople become great salespeople. These systems generate information so the follow up can be executed and managed. Then, customers are not forgotten.

The Sale: When a sale is made, it is critical to get it entered in a timely and 100% accurate fashion. Delays in sale entry cause inventory counts to be off, resulting in all sorts of potential problems. The sale must be entered with the correct quantities, location, amounts, tax, items, salesperson, shipping method, addresses, payment terms, and special instructions. IPad and PC tablets are great ways to get the sale entered in a timely and professional manner.

Just telling your people to do this does not always make it happen. Every link in the chain must be managed. One purpose of management is to inspect what you expect. Without inspecting work and repetitive training, there will be errors and customers will suffer. At the end of each day's business, review all sales for accuracy.

Daily Cash Reconciling: Perfect control of daily cash in your system is required. Forget manual day sheets unless you are committed to being a pen and paper operation. Every business software system includes a report to review daily cash receipts. At the end of each day or the following morning, run a cash report for the cash, checks, credit cards, and finance payments received into your system. Compare it against the physical cash, checks, and credit card totals collected. If there is a discrepancy, either someone made a mistake entering a receipt, the money never came in, or it is somewhere else. Rectify all issues immediately. This process should take under 20 minutes per day for even large operations.

If Merchandise Is Taken From Stock

When merchandise is sold, it is either taken from stock or special ordered. If assigned against stock, the correct location of the items in inventory must be attached in the system. For example, if you have one item located on the floor and one of the same items located in your warehouse, the entry person needs to make sure the customer's sale is assigned appropriately to inventory.

After choosing the right item location the date of the pick up or delivery should be set in the system. If the date is unknown, it should say ASAP or Not Set.

Take-With: In situations where customers take products with them, a receipt should be generated upon taking possession of the goods. As a rule of thumb, whenever merchandise comes into a building or leaves a building, there needs to be a receipt. During the sale entry of a take-with item, the sale can be finalized at that time. The merchandise moves out of the "books" and the customer's account is invoiced. If not fully paid there is a receivable balance. Otherwise, the customer's account is $0 and sales history is recorded.

Pick-Up: A pick-up is when a customer comes in to get the merchandise after the original sale. The customer signs for the merchandise. Payments are accepted where necessary. The signed receipt is retained and forwarded to the office by the end of the day.

Delivery: If merchandise is in stock and the customer wishes delivery, the undelivered sale should be scheduled for shipping appropriately in the system. This date acts as a communication tool between various departments and your customer. It allows the salesperson to know when the customer expects the merchandise; the warehouse to know when to get the inventory ready; the office to know when the sale is expected to be invoiced.

If Stock Needs To Be Ordered

Special Order Purchasing For Customers: I am a believer in point-of-sale entry. That means that the sale is entered in front of the customer at the time of the sale. Operations that can't do this have to rely on interpretation of various handwritings at some point after the sale. If a customer requires a special order, it makes sense to have them agree to the specific details, by involving them in the process at the point of sale, as well. After sales are entered each day, purchase orders can be "generated" automatically for sales that are not assigned against in-stock merchandise. The POs should be double checked by salespeople, the purchasing staff, or both before being placed with the vendor. The PO should include the customer's name and sale number.

Stock POs: The other type of purchase order is for stock. Like customer POs, stock POs should be entered in your system at the time of ordering. Never hand write them or place orders verbally with a vendor representative. One of the biggest breaks in the chain of operations occurs here. Someone tells the rep to order some merchandise and the PO never gets entered. When the merchandise arrives, the warehouse has no idea what to do with it. Enter the PO in real time and this won't happen to you.

The PO number is your master merchandise tracking number and all orders must be placed with a system PO number. Require that vendors use this same reference number.

Purchase Follow-Up: POs should be acknowledged. The estimated arrival dates should be updated. The costs should be adjusted. The accuracy of the order should be reviewed. Unless an order is transmitted via EDI (electronic data interchange) or through a vendor's system online, there is a chance of error on entry. The acknowledgement gives you time to correct errors. In integrated systems, this process also updates the salespeople's CRM info so that they can communicate with their customers regarding order status. As well, expected arrival times for new stock are known.

Receiving Preparation: Insist that all vendors schedule your incoming freight. Get them to send a packing list via email prior to the freight's arrival. This enables your warehouse crew to be ready for the truckload. The appropriate staff can be scheduled. Bar code labels can be preprinted and organized. The dock can be cleared. It will not get jammed by multiple unexpected containers arriving at the same time. You will be ready.

Receiving: One person should direct the receiving crew. This person needs to have all the bar code labels organized on a large receiving table by the dock. After a crew member moves the merchandise from the truck, he/she needs to stop so that the receiving director can scan the label and stick it on the product. If the warehouse has a wireless system the quantities in the system will be updated immediately. If the warehouse uses a batch bar code system, the quantities from the scanner should be uploaded to the system immediately after the physical receiving is complete. Either way, the merchandise information is updated fast for everyone in the organization to see in real time. Manual entry of receiving, sometime after the fact, is less efficient.

Your system should inform the receiving crew if merchandise is for stock, floor display, or a special order. Stock inventory can be moved and scanned to any available rack location. Efficient warehouses with effective employees use locator systems that allow merchandise to be easily put away and easily found. This allows for the best use of space and time.

If the merchandise is not on display, your operating chain should include a function to identify items that should be moved to a showroom. Quick operations will have a designated floor transfer area in their warehouses.

A cross dock system can be put in place for special orders. Like the merchandise to display system, merchandise to be delivered can have a special area. Again, this can speed up the process of getting the merchandise in and out.

Any paperwork including bills of lading, packing lists, freight invoices, and receiving registers should be organized by the truckload and forwarded promptly to accounts payable.

Delivery Scheduling: Sales can be scheduled for delivery by one person or several people. Either way, customers should be contacted fast to set a date. The faster your customers are booked, the faster is your revenue cycle. Other than the date and time of delivery, all relevant notes and COD requirements should be dealt with on scheduling. Cutoff product levels should be established by piece, cube, and/or stop. The goal is to schedule to capacity each day. Cutoff times also need to be in place so that the manager knows when to start pulling product.

Even small mom and pop operations benefit greatly from doing it this way as opposed to pulling a paper sale, writing a delivery, and sticking it on a clip board.

Delivery Picking and Preparation: At cutoff time, picking information is generated. In large operations with mechanical pickers, racks, and levels, it is best to pick by aisle as opposed to picking by customer. In this way the crew does not go back and forth, revisiting the same warehouse areas. In smaller, non-racked warehouses with limited space, it may be faster to pick by the customer.

The cutoff time to start picking will depend on the average amount of preparation that is required to get the merchandise ready for delivery. This can be anywhere between a half day to two days.

Operations that spend more quality time on merchandise preparation and inspection have happier customers and fewer after delivery-related service issues.

All merchandise that goes in and out of a building needs a signature of receipt. Delivery receipts, therefore, need to be generated for the date of delivery. This can be done on paper or on a tablet / iPad-type device that allows for a customer signature.

Deliveries should be routed using a mapping application. These programs allow for big savings in people hours, customer time, and driving costs. Once the route is mapped, the customer can be texted, called, or emailed with the delivery time window.

Finalizing Delivery: Customers sign for merchandise upon delivery. If they sign electronically, some apps can auto-finalize the sale in the IT system. For companies that use paper delivery receipts, these receipts and any money collected should be submitted to the office as soon as the truck returns at the end of the day. Either method works well.

Businesses that have a broken link here tend to have open sales that sit in their system for long periods of time. This leaves them exposed to theft, collection problems, financial inaccuracy, and unpaid sales tax issues.

Accounts Payable: Each day, information should arrive from the inventory receiving manager. This info should be filed as "Merchandise received, waiting on invoice entry".

Each day, merchandise and freight invoices arrive from vendors. This should be filed as "Invoice not entered, waiting on receiving".

Even if an invoice arrives before a shipment, it should only be entered when there is a verification of receiving the goods. At that time, the costs can be adjusted. Actual landed costs are reflected in the cost of goods. Without this link, costs, as well as product pricing and gross margins may become inaccurate.

On accounts payable entry, the receiving and invoices should be matched and then filed as "Entered, to be paid".

Expense invoices follow a much simpler route. Just enter them when the mail is opened. Don't let invoices stack up on someone's desk without being entered. If this occurs, your debt situation would be understated - then on the date when all the entry happens, you may be shocked by how much money you suddenly owe.

Check Writing Process: Check runs are often prepared weekly. Once per week, on Wednesday, for example, review an account payables open aging or cash requirements by due date report. Depending on your cash situation, decide on what you want, or don't want to pay. Make the selections in your system. On Thursday, print and sign the checks. Staple the office check stub to the invoice. File as "Vendor Paid".

Ledger and Financial Statements: In an integrated ERP (Enterprise Resource Planning) system, all information from sales, cash, accounts receivable, inventory, accounts payable, and payroll end up in the general ledger. Journal entries are made automatically to the proper account. For systems that are not integrated, journal entries should be done as the activity occurs.

Do your bank reconciliation online daily or a few times per week. This allows you to catch any additional charges that need to be entered. It also helps catch cash errors that occurred in accounts payable or bank deposits. It is faster and keeps your information system up to date.

If your financial statements are set up properly in advance, you should be able to just push a button each month for your master business performance reports. You will automatically get:

Profit and Loss Statements – this will show your sales, cost of goods, gross margin, operating costs, and net income for various profit centers.

Balance Sheet – this will show your general business health as far as what you own and what you owe.

Cash Flow Statement – this will show your cash position at the beginning of the period, why it changed, and your cash position at the end of the period.

There are many operational links that are critical for the health of your business. Strong functional links produce strong information. This efficient chain allows your employees to better serve your customers. Weak links or constraints deter good information. They make business difficult. Examine your operations chain and ask these questions:

"Does it make sense to do it this way?"

"Are we doing it this way because we always have?"

"How can we exploit and fix our constraining weak links?"

"What actions can we take to keep on improving?"

4. OPERATIONAL BOTTLENECKS AND PRODUCTIVITY CONSTRAINTS

Have you ever wondered why some businesses seem to run smoothly while others seem to live in a constant state of chaos?

I see this all the time in the field.

Some operations churn along like well-oiled machines. They produce consistently decent sales volumes for their space. They can handle all their customer traffic properly. Managers are proactive. Purchase orders are placed and received without issue. Deliveries go off without a hitch. Inventory counts are always right. Accounts payable is current. Financial Statements are correct and timely each month. Customer service issues seldom occur and when they do the customer comes out happy in the end. Employees truly enjoy their workplace. Cash flow is good.

Other operations live on the seat of their pants. They move from fighting one fire to the next. Managers are reactive. They spend their time and energy focusing on the biggest problem of the day. Retail traffic and sales projections are a mystery. Sometimes there is not enough trained salespeople to handle the customer load properly. Other times their salespeople are just sitting around staring at the door. Purchase orders occasionally arrive wrong. Merchandise on the floor is old and inventory quantities are often incorrect. Damages occur and customer service issues are a problem. There are many complaints to deal with. Payables get behind. Financial statements and management reports are unreliable. Employee are stressed. Cash flow is poor.

The difference between smooth-run and chaotic-run operations often are the bottlenecks. A bottleneck is a slowdown in business operations in one or more areas. Work piles up in the bottleneck area and becomes unproductive. All the business functions after the bottleneck are effected due to the less than optimal management of workflow.

A case in point; a particular operation's salespeople were having trouble serving their customers properly because they didn't have access to quality inventory information. Salespeople would actually call the warehouse to check to see if there was stock available. Then the warehouse had to physically look for stock and call back the salesperson. Many customers would just leave. This resulted in both the sales and the warehouse people having to do more work and they got less sales for the business. We found that there was a bottleneck in their inventory control and IT communications. This led to issues "downstream" in their sales department.

Bottlenecks are caused by constraints in productivity. A constraint is some inefficiency in process or ineffective use of resources. To continue the case above, we found that the inefficiency was caused by the warehouse transferring merchandise from location to location without following the proper procedures in their IT system. Thus, there was a breakdown in their inventory control. They also were ineffective since they didn't use scanning equipment. They used less timely and less accurate hand written and manual key methods instead of bar coding to reduce their human error factor. The result of their inaccurate inventory was the productivity constraint that caused their operational bottleneck.

Having a smooth-run operation is a prerequisite for maximizing sales, profits and cash flow. This is because better use of resources means that less costs get assigned to making the operation work. Operations with lots of constraints and bottlenecks tend to add more costs to deal with their inadequacies. They put money in the wrong place.

Examples: If an operation can't seem to get financial statements out on time, they might add extra people to get things processed by a deadline. If the distribution center can't find merchandise quick enough for transport, they might hire more workers to help look. If product is not being reordered timely and stock-outs often occur, extra unnecessary buffer stock may be added, driving inventory cost up.

This Theory of Constraints (TOC) was first introduced by Dr. Eliyahu Goldratt promoting the management practice that, "The goal is not to save money but to make money." The basic premise with dealing with constraints to improve an organization are:

1. Find the Constraint.
2. Figure out how to "exploit" or improve the constraint.
3. Subordinate everything else. Get all other areas of the organization to support the goal of improving.
4. Elevate the Constraint. Execute the improvements necessary to break the bottleneck.
5. Review and monitor. If the constraint is still there, go back to step 1. If the bottleneck is broken, look to other areas to improve. There is always a constraint to improve on.

To assist you in finding your operational bottlenecks so that you can eliminate constraints, I have listed some signs for you to consider:

Possible Signs of Bottlenecks and Constraints

Sales:

- Too busy to follow-up with customers
- Lots of idle time
- Mistakes in data entry

- Taking too long to enter sales orders
- Poor or no CRM data: close rates x traffic x average ticket
- Missing sales goals, repeatedly
- No sales quotes or old sales quotes in the IT system
- Lots of split commission sales
- Excess discounting
- Few add-ons to sales orders resulting in low average ticket
- Too much time spent on customer service issues
- Slow daily cash-out process
- Unstructured or non-existent sales meetings
- Complaining

Purchasing:

- Poor merchandise mix
- Over-inventory
- Stock-outs of hot selling items
- Poor lead times and transport issues
- Unfavorable vendor terms
- Costing issues – merchandise and freight-in
- Margin drift

Merchandise Management:

- Unorganized floor and display issues
- Missing price points in the merchandise line-up
- Odd ball pricing
- No group pricing
- Too much old, non-selling merchandise in the floor
- Everything is on sale or nothing is on sale
- Merchandise that is not displayed anywhere, yet in-stock

Inventory Control:

- Employees hand writing things down and data entering later
- Inventory out of location

- Status mistakes
- Quantity errors
- Manual or hand written sold tags in the warehouse
- Re-wrapped merchandise in the warehouse

Distribution:

- Large number of incoming customer calls
- High shipping and delivery costs with respect to incoming revenue
- Returned merchandise
- Service issues
- Damages
- Crowded docks
- Large amount of undelivered and unscheduled sales orders
- Slow picking and prep processes
- Interdepartmental complaints
- Routine less than full delivery trucks
- Overuse of equipment and vehicles

Accounting / Management:

- Poor financial reporting
- An inaccurate balance sheet
- Inventory costing issues
- Over use of spreadsheets
- Blaming things on IT
- Delivered sales still showing as written sales
- Takes a long time to do commissions and payroll
- Too much staff for sales volume
- Month end is always a rush
- Late financial statements
- Poor reconciliation procedures
- Creeping miscellaneous expense
- High employee stress level and turnover

- Constant issue resolution and firefighting
- Average or low profitability overall

Solutions to constraints should be tailored specifically to your organization. There is no one size fits all. Team dynamics and internal processes will vary from one business to the next. Personalities, abilities, IT, and management structure in your organization should be looked at in determining the best approach.

I believe in focusing on one thing at a time. It could be a mistake for you to try to improve several major areas area of the business at once. After identifying the best area to improve your business, define your strategy. Get all team members on-board. Define the specific tactics to accomplish your desired results. Measure your progress, adjust and fine-tune until you succeed. Don't stop. Keep advancing. The best operations in the world commit to continuous improvement.

5. THE 5 SMART STEPS

I have used the 5 SMART Steps to improve the cash flow of countless companies. It is an acronym that was originally thought of by the retail software & solutions company, PROFITsystems Inc., to help their clients prosper. The 5 SMART steps are merchandising, sales, and marketing focused. They are field-proven to produce greater sales and higher profits. Mastering their implementation is essential to retail operational success.

Let's simplify things. You make money by selling inventory and services. You lose money by buying inventory that does not sell and by incurring expenses associated with non-saleable inventory.

5 "SMART" Steps:

Spot your best sellers.

Maintain your winners.

Auto identify and take action on dogs.

Reward high gross margin sales.

Target market your best customers.

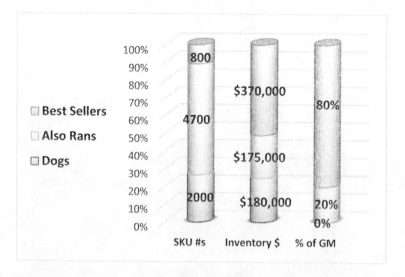

SMART Step 1 - Spot Your Best Sellers!

The chart above represents a blend of SKUs (items for sale). These numbers are typical for many operations. The top shaded area represents best sellers or the winning items. The middle shaded areas are the also-ran items or the lukewarm performing items. And the bottom shaded areas are unproductive inventory or the dogs. In this case, 800 items with a value of $370,000 at cost produced 80% of the gross margin dollars. This is the 80/20 principle in action. I guarantee that if we analyze your SKU base, it will be similar to this in percentage. Most of your margin dollars will come from a minority of your SKUs.

The chart also shows that 4,700 also-ran items had a value of $175,000 at cost and produced the remaining 20% of gross margin dollars. Also-rans are either best sellers that died out, dogs that finally sold, or new items becoming best sellers!

On the bottom you can see that 2,000 items were dogs. They represented $180,000 in inventory invested. They produced $0. The definition of a dog is an item that produces 0 or negative gross margin dollars.

This highlights the extreme importance of Step 1. Spot the best sellers. This merchandise is your gold. You need to know all of these items, fast, and make sure that all managers and all employees know them as well. Without keeping tabs on best sellers you may never even know the gold that you may have had. Here is how to spot these items:

• Each month, generate a ranking of items underneath their respective categories and vendors. Sort by gross margin volume produced for the prior 3 months. This keeps the analysis consistent and routine.

• Assign a 1, 2, or 3 ranking to the best-selling items to represent the best of the best (#1), next of the best (#2), and rest of the best (#3). This establishes priority for you to follow (some IT systems can do this for you automatically).

• Post a top 100 item list in your lunch room.

• Have all managers educate the employees, especially salespeople, on where to find these items on the showroom floor and how to promote them to your customers. These items have the highest demand and produce the most profit. They are proven to be more "natural" to sell. Some employees will know some of this product already, but few will know all of it. There are just too many items with constantly changing lifecycles.

• If you are a custom order business, identify your best sellers by the style model that produces highest margin dollars even though details can come in many combinations.

• Analyze and educate every month. Don't stop. Your inventory is in constant motion.

Knowing and measuring is the first step to success. What is measured can be improved. Do it with a system. No human can possibly keep track of the constantly changing dynamics of thousands of items. Those managers that continually focus on what works tend to produce greater results. Those that operate using a seat-of-their pants mentality or who rely on a "recent memory system", leave A LOT of dollars on the table.

SMART Step 2: Maintain Your Winners!

It is tough to sell something if your customer can't see it, right? That's obvious. If you agree with SMART Step 1: that best sellers produce the lion's share of the profits and that knowing them is critical, then, **why do operations run out of these items?**

The best performing businesses rarely run out of their best merchandise. These stores maintain their winners in stock 95%+ of the time. Thus their sales from these items are maximized. Average stores have their best sellers in stock about 85% of the time. Underperforming operations lose sales due to their lower percentage of in stock days.

Best seller "stock-outs" is the costliest of all inventory management challenges. Suppose that you run out of an item that typically sells 10 units per month for an average margin of $750. If you run out of it for 2 months, what is your loss? $15,000 in margin. $30,000 in sales at 50% Gross Margin. And – less than happy salespeople. And that is just one item! Say that happens to 50 items per year. What then? That's a massive loss in sales volume that is hidden from your P&L (Profit and Loss Statement).

To remedy this type of situation, minimize your stock-out loss and maximize your profits, track these elements on your individual winning items:

• In stock and out of stock days.

• Sales – Average units per month, actual units per 6 months and per year.

• Merchandising – Quantity displayed on floor. Quantity, in transit. Quantity damaged.

• Lead time on average.

• Quantity in stock available for sale.

• Available quantity on order for sale and ETA (Estimated time of arrival) date.

• GM, GMROI, ROI – Gross margin produced and the return on investment of the item. (GMROI is explained in detail in the Inventory section of this book)

• Cost – Raw cost (cost before freight), landed cost (cost after freight), and average cost (average cost of landed inventory).

• Current selling price and expected margin at that price point.

From this item information you can maintain your winners better:

• Estimate when you will run out of an item.

• Reorder the appropriate quantity at the right time considering lead time, rate of sale, and stock levels.

• Display the item if not displayed.

• Nail down the item if it is a best seller (do not sell the showroom display model).

• Service damaged items and seek vendor credits where required.

• Fulfill a customer's purchase order sooner if there is currently available merchandise.

• Do not over order. Do not under order.

• See costing increases with respect to vendors and freight carriers.

• Check price points and margins at the most recent costing – you will gain a huge amount of extra margin if you do this right.

Just in time inventory (JIT) supply without stock-outs produce high returns. Maintain your winners and your sales and profits will increase.

SMART Step #3: Auto-identify and Take Action on Dogs!

Auto-identifying your dogs means using your IT (Information Technology) systems to help you find your non-selling inventory. I know what some of you are thinking, "I know my dogs. I don't need a computer to tell me what items are not making me any money." That thought can only be true if you either carry few inventory SKUs or have a team of people tracking each single SKU on a daily basis. Operations with at least a few hundred thousand dollars in inventory at cost can have thousands of SKUs. They can cover over 20 merchandise categories, and will have many more vendors. You need to automatically query your merchandise database to flush out non-performers. This enables you to take quick action to increase turns and maximize gross margin. Here is how you can do it:

• Set up an inventory aging schedule that will define your markdown levels.

• Create up to six aging periods in the schedule.

• For each aging period, assign a number of days aged and a desired markdown discount. A typical markdown aging for a non-seasonal business could be every sixty days. Six periods would be 60 days, 120 days, 180 days, 240 days, 300 days, and 360 days.

• Query your inventory data once per month for all merchandise that is not a best seller. This will allow you to auto-identify your Dogs.

Once you have the information, take action. The Dogs are not going to disappear just because they have been identified. Below, you can see example actions to take once merchandise drifts into subsequent aging levels. Actions can be discounting, re-display, spiffing the salespeople, a marketing opportunity, or a combination of actions. As the merchandise gets older, take increasingly decisive actions.

If, you had a piece of merchandise on the floor for a year, would you return it to the vendor if you could? One hundred percent of my clients answer, "Yes!" So, selling a small minority of inventory at or below cost is the same thing – and, a customer will be getting a fantastic deal!

Sample Markdown Aging Schedule				
Inventory Markdown Level	Type of Merchandise	Days Aged	Associated Discount and/or Actions	Approximate % of Total Inventory in Period for efficiency
Current	New or good selling items	Under 60 days	Display, never discount, nail down	70% of inventory value
Level 1	Newly aged	60-120 days	10% discount and/or redisplay	12% of inventory value
Level 2	Official Dogs	121-180 days	20% discount and/or un-nail	7% of inventory value
Level 3	Very stagnant	181-240 days	30% discount and/or spiff	5% of inventory value
Level 4	Emergency	241-300 days	40% discount and/or internet clearance	3% of inventory value
Level 5	Give away	301-360 days	50% discount and/or donate, prize items	2% of inventory value
Level 6	The worst, Garbage	Over 360 days	60% discount or write-off scrap	Under 1% of inventory value

The next question I get is, "Don't these markdowns hurt my margins?" Answer: They actually make your margins better. You get a higher margin sooner as opposed to getting a lesser margin later.

SMART Step #4: Reward High Gross Margin Sales!

One system of paying commissions stands above the rest - variable sliding based on gross margin percentage. This system aligns the goals of profitability for the company with the salespeople's goals of making the most commission.

I have witnessed immediate 3%-8% jumps in gross margin percentage overall in switching to this method. That translates to a huge increase in bottom line profitability.

So if you currently pay out the same percentage of sales regardless of the margin the merchandise is sold at, this may be the fastest and easiest way you will achieve a higher gross margin %. Your Return on Inventory Investment could sky rocket. This is also true of operations that supposedly don't discount.

Here is how it works:

If a salesperson sells something at a higher gross margin percentage, you will pay a corresponding higher commission percentage.

If a salesperson sells something at a lower gross margin percentage, you will pay a corresponding lower commission percentage.

If a salesperson sells something at an average gross margin percentage, you will pay an average commission percentage.

Moving to Variable Rate Commissions

1. Figure out your percentage of commission on sales for average margin sales. By doing this, if nothing changes, everyone gets paid the same and your expense is the same. Refer to the following example. Note that if an item is sold at a 45% gross margin, there is a 5% commission paid. So, for a $1,000 item, $50 is paid in commission. Very average. Nothing really changes.

Sample Variable Sliding Commission Schedule
(Variable rate based on gross margin, commissionable on selling price)

Gross Margin %	Commission %	Commission Due on $1000 example
55%	9.0%	$90
54%	8.6%	$86
53%	8.2%	$82
52%	7.8%	$78
51%	7.4%	$74
50%	7.0%	$70
49%	6.6%	$66
48%	6.2%	$62
47%	5.8%	$58
46%	5.4%	$54
45%	5.0%	$50
44%	4.6%	$46
43%	4.2%	$42
42%	3.8%	$38
41%	3.4%	$34
40%	3.0%	$30

2. Set a high gross margin percentage and related high commission percentage. Selling an item at 55% produces a 9% commission, or $90 for a $1,000 item. The salesperson will be pleased because they make an extra 4% commission. Your company will by very happy because it makes an extra 10% in GM and extra 6% in profits!

3. Set a low gross margin percentage and related low commission percentage. The range between the top commission and the bottom commission needs to be at least 5% for variable sliding to work because the incentive is not as strong with anything less than that. In the example, the low commission percentage is 3% at a 40% gross margin sale. If you have a working markdown system in place this

Final

will be a minority of items. The salesperson is less likely to negotiate discounts. They will also STOP bugging the sales manager to lower the price, saving you, the salesperson, and the customer time. Instead of price selling, salespeople will start to using value selling techniques. **So, this also translates into better customer service.**

4. Set it up right. Do your math right. Make your schedule easy to understand. It is important that everyone fully understands the incentive system.

5. Roll it out. Don't be scared. Tell your salespeople you want to make them partners in your profitability and share more of the gains with them. This is a profit sharing plan. It is a raise! And, for those of you who want to test it first, tell your salespeople that you will run the new system in conjunction with the old way of doing things. Then tell them you will pay them on whichever way makes them the most commission. That will most likely last for one month and the old way will be ancient history.

So, now you know how to spot best sellers and maintain them better. You know how to get rid of dogs faster. And you are going to make a higher gross margin overall doing it!

To gain the biggest benefit you need the highest traffic possible. If you can increase traffic, while practicing the first four SMART steps, you will maximize the impact that the SMART steps have on your overall profitability. The greatest cash flow will be achieved. The final SMART step helps you increase traffic while managing your merchandise and sales force better.

Smart Step #5: Target Customers in Your Database!

The SMART Steps presented so far, cannot be implemented properly without solid retail traffic. The 80/20 principle states that the high majority of your revenue is produced by a minority of your customers. This is not an assumption or guess. Analyze your sales for the past five years and rank them by customer volume. You will likely see the same thing.

That is why knowing your best customers and treating them like gold is so important to business operations. These customers are, in fact, a gold mine. This step is about properly mining the customer gold mine for repeat business.

First off, this elite group must be treated extra special. Don't just blast advertise to them. Your best customers should be part of your "VIP club" and receive special notices, gifts, birthday wishes, and invitations to private functions.

Segmenting this group separately from the bulk of your database will allow for better communication. If you have 50,000 people in your database and you want to have a cocktail party to introduce a new product line, do you want to send out 50,000 invitations? I say no. With this type of event, it is not all about traffic numbers. It's about the right traffic. You will be better off sending 1,000 personal emails generated from your salespeople. When your best customers come to the private event, you will actually be able to spend some time with them and properly determine their needs. That's better than a showroom full of discount seekers, right?

Other than hosting a private VIP sale, there are other key targeted messages that should be sent via email, text, or snail mail to your customers. The purpose is to touch your customer more often with a real reason rather than using the same old holiday weekend promo. Remember, these messages should not go out to your entire data base. You must segment for relevancy. Here are some examples:

"Thank you for visiting our store. Do you have any other questions?"

This message can be sent to anyone who gives you their information, whether they bought or not. It encourages customers to think of you first while they are shopping around.

"Price quote and special information attached."

Send a message after a quote has been written up with all the necessary information. This is a great follow-up tool. The more quotes you give, the higher your sales will be – if you follow up.

"Thank you for your purchase! Here is a copy of your sales receipt."

This message should be sent after each sale. This gives customers a contact name and number should they have any questions or need something else.

"Special order update inside."

Every customer wants to know the status of their order. Send them a message like this and it will save them time and show that you are really taking care of them.

"Your merchandise is ready. Request your delivery or pick up."

Many customers now prefer to do business via email rather than telephone. People don't like wasting time with telephone tag. Give your customer the gift of convenience. Use their preferred method of contact.

"Delivery reminder with date and time."

Send a reminder that goes right into your customer's smart phone. They will see that you are an innovative business

"Take our Satisfaction Survey and get a gift card."

After the delivery or pick up, send them a three question survey. You will build valuable information over time.

"Help with your next purchase."

If you can get customer information on next purchase desires, contact them and give some ideas. Use both email and the cell numbers for contact.

"Suggested related ideas."

You can contact people that bought products that have complimentary items. For example, a suit may have matching shoes. Or, a table may have a matching rug.

"We miss you – here is a gift!"

Search your past purchase information by last date of purchase. For big customers who have not visited in a while, send a note with a gift that they can pick up at the showroom.

"Locals night only."

It may be a local community that brings people together. Divide your audience by their zip codes and send special messages.

"Product demonstration."

This may be one for your VIP list. Why not educate your customers on your product or service with a fun-type demo?

"Happy birthday gift!"

Most people love to be remembered on special occasions. It's pretty much a guarantee read.

One common question, I get is, "Isn't this too many messages?"

Not if done right. If you target properly and do it professionally, it will work. Touching your customers more equals higher traffic. On the flip side, if you send the same tired messages to everyone, they will appear to be blasts and get fewer results. Be relevant.

Bottom line: Get to know your customers. Use targeted mediums such as email, mobile phone, text, Facetime, Facebook to do so. Mass media is advertising. This is relationship marketing. Targeting allows you to focus on developing long term relationships on a more personal level with the right people. When a customer becomes a friend then they become a customer for life.

Executing and improving on the 5 "SMART" Steps will propel you to new levels of sales, profitability and cash flow:

Spot your best sellers.

Maintain your winners.

Auto identify and take action on dogs.

Reward high gross margin sales.

Target market your best customers.

6. GET YOUR SALES BACK

I was analyzing the traffic data of a retail store recently. I cross referenced this data with their advertising spend data over three years. I observed that their traffic had significantly declined while their advertising expenditure remained constant. Sales fell and expenses went up – not a good combination.

Over the span of these three years they saw sales trend down and they continually reacted by searching for a promotion that would "hit big". Occasionally they did find one. But, not often enough.

They were bewildered, thinking, "What was happening and how could we turn our business around?"

This operation was relying on traffic (customer visits) as the sole driver of sales and traditional advertising as the sole driver of traffic. They surmised that if their TV, newspaper, and radio advertising ads brought in the same number of people each time they had a promotion, then their sales would be relatively similar. Their close rate and average sale did not fluctuate much – so it was logical that ad-driven traffic was the ultimate answer. However, the mix of their normal media channels just did not bring in the same number of customers as it once did.

They thought if they advertised a bit more, sales would eventually get back to "normal". New customers would eventually answer their call and come in, right? That would have possibly worked, if it was not for two major occurrences: increased competition and consumer media on-demand.

Increased competition through manufacturer, national branded chains and internet retailers brought an increase in inventory and active retail sales space to their area. Consumers had more options. The population in their trade area did not go up significantly, while more stores were advertising to the same audience.

At the same time, traditional media was becoming less effective due to media that was consumed on-demand. The digitization of media put the controls in the hands of the audience. That audience could now dictate which messages they would allow marketers to show them and when they would consume that media. Radio now had satellite, TV had DVR and Apple TV, newspapers had web content, the yellow pages had Google, and direct mail had email marketing.

People more and more were getting their media when and where they wanted it.

The old methods now produced: Declining in-store traffic per dollars spent. Declining in-store sales due to reliance on traditional media traffic.

So, what was answer for this operation?

Adapt and Adopt to the new: Get sales back by following the path of the digitally-minded consumer.

Here are some actions that this particular company executed to offset the reduced impact of traditional marketing to eventually get traffic and sales numbers back to decent levels:

- They analyzed their current marketing strategy (ROI (return on investment) on advertising) to determine if it was right for their tech-dependent 21st century customer.
- They implemented a host of digital media solutions. This included various elements:

- o A web site that served its purpose (i.e. It actually brought traffic into their physical store – imagine that?)
- o Search Engine Optimization & Marketing (SEO & SEM) that was right for them. They communicated their message through properly placed key words and relevant search messages.
- o A blog that provided valuable and current info to customers. They were able to build a following and spread their wings on the web through self-publishing of dynamic content.
- o E-newsletters that were creative (and not spam or blasts). They included information that was customer lifestyle targeted. They cut out communicating through Ad-Speak.
- o Real-time instant-messaging for customer assistance. It was simple. They just put a link on their site that said, "Need Help?" "Click Here". Instantly customers got connected to sales representatives.
- o Social media paid advertising. They realized that Facebook was a segue to specifically targeting customers with relevant messages. For instance, they customized different messages for married women between the ages of 35-50, than messages for single men between 25-40.
- They reallocated increasing funds in their marketing budget: shifted increasingly more $ from traditional media to digital media as their ROI dictated.
- They still used traditional media but chose to dominate 1 traditional media-type rather than spread dollars thinly across all traditional medias. In this case they chose Broadcast TV and dominated the morning news leading to the weekend.
- They found new media partners and let go of old commissioned agents.
- They modified their business model to focus on their customer rather than themself.

- They re-defined their selling system. They documented and improved each step of their value chain from the time the customer first saw their message until after the purchase.
- They got the right people on their team and the wrong ones off. (Get on the bus or get off approach).
- They switched their focus from a traffic only focus. They put more emphasis on average sales and close rates.
- They got a capable Sales floor Leader.
- They followed-up with all customers better. They now used phone calls, email, text, Facetime, Skype. They communicated however their customers wished to communicate. They built better relationships as a result.
- They analyzed and tracked all important data. This enabled them to make changes faster.

Executing similar elements into your business will allow you to provide a higher level of customer service, achieve a higher average sale and close rate, and yes, increase traffic.

There are only two choices with the digital age: Jump in, change with your customers and enjoy the ride, or cut costs and learn to live off lower traffic. The choice is clear – have fun with it!

7. CHARACTERISTICS OF BUSINESS OPERATORS

Truly, people in retail are some of the most fun and down to earth business people. This has been my personal experience for most of the thousands of people that I have worked with - whether they were good, average, or poor business operators.

When I first was published several years ago, my editor said to me, "I want you to write about what people are asking you in the field. Write about common challenges or questions that they have." Remembering this made me think of the two most common questions that I am asked by business owners:

(1) "What do you see the best operators do?"

(2) "What common mistakes do you see in poor operations?"

Everyone wants to know what is working, right? And, of course, you all want to avoid the pitfalls. I believe that the heart and soul of retail is the independent entrepreneurs. At one time I thought that would change. Now I believe that this will remain the norm for some time. Of course there are the Wal-Marts, the Home Depots and the Ikeas of the world. That won't change. But, at the same time smaller regional operations will continue to exist to provide alternate products and services to the corporate chains. That said, only some will thrive – those that seek continual self-improvement.

The most profitable independent businesses have teams that work well together and have team members that complement each other's skills. They never stop pushing themselves to become better. Their management and operations are more customer focused than their competition.

On the other hand, independent businesses that don't adopt this business ethos, tend to stagnate and have lower profitability. The poor operators are reactionary, and manage by "the seat of their pants". These managers need to improve themselves to survive. Legacy does not extend into the future.

Now, back to the best. Another trait of successful operations is the company's ability to innovate. They implement the most current management systems and procedures so that they can keep a constant finger on the pulse of their businesses. Example, if sales go down, they know why and can adjust quickly.

They don't just complain that, "It's slow." That means nothing in itself. If cash flow is up or down, they know exactly why. The best have decent cash flows, even during recessions. Poor businesses take excessive loans (from banks, vendors, and customers) even in the boom years.

Innovation flows through all aspects of great operations. Good managers implement best practices sooner and try new ideas.

Some additional characteristics of the best retailers:

- There is complete usage of an integrated software system with minimal manual processes.

- They don't waste time. They run lean.

- They pay better for fewer well-trained and motivated people.

- They have a web page that is a profit center and it provides leads.

- They control their marketing. The best stores realize that the most effective advertisements come from their own people. They focus on communication and customer follow up.

- They have 99% inventory accuracy and they do this via bar coding. There is no other way.

- They use mobile devices to look up inventory and enter sales. This technology allows salespeople to serve customers throughout the entire selling process.

- They use innovative engagement techniques to guide customers and salespeople through the buying process. For example, an innovative running shoe store might use a treadmill run stride test to sell more shoes. Or, a mattress business may use a comfort profile to sell more beds.

- They use IT (information technology) systems to track consumer behavior so that they can offer better products and services in the future.

Operations that are making mistakes often are making the biggest one of all: Doing the same thing over and over with diminishing results. They are subject to the fluctuating conditions of the marketplace. They have little control over their business.

Great retail operators really understand GMROI ($ Annual GM / $ Inventory). (I will explain GMROI in detail in the Inventory Section of this book). They implement aspects of the acronym "SMART" steps. (writing #5)

The smartest people think they are not the smartest people and have a lot to learn. These people get advice. They are probably reading this now. The best of the best don't hunker down and live in a cage in their store. They belong to performance groups, attend seminars, and have their favorite business consultants, coaches, and advisors who help them implement change. They are networkers.

These people get things done! They decide. They commit. They don't make false promises. They ooze integrity. When the best say they are going to do something – they JUST DO IT. It is hard to stop them. They are Entrepreneurs!

Businesses that falter are the ones that cannot make decisions. They are worriers. They do not take risks and as a result, do not realize big rewards.

Never wait for the economy! Continue to seek ways to improve your situation, whatever it is. That is what you CAN control. Watch for opportunities and seize them when they come by.

If you wish to be greater than you are now, you must take steps to change who you are now.

8. RELATIONSHIP MARKETING

Improve the way you do business, strengthen the bonds with your customers and sell more!

How much do you spend on advertising every year? Well most operations, that I visit, spend around 5-8% of sales. Wow – That means that, if you do $5 million top line, you are putting $250,000 to $400,000 toward media costs. Ok – that's fine if it is producing increasing or even stable leads. But, many businesses have experienced declining traffic, while advertising dollars have remained similar. This has forced the ratio to go over 8% of sales in many cases!

Traditional multimedia approaches are simply not producing the same results. Like in Spencer Johnson's famous novel, Who Moved My Cheese; the cheese, which could represent consumer behavior, has moved. It's time to adapt to the change that has occurred.

Your customers are very busy and have more choice than ever. They don't need to open the junk mail, to look in the yellow pages, to listen to the local radio channel, to watch TV commercials or to read the local newspaper. Now, they get the info that they want, when they want it, ON DEMAND. They go to their favorites on the internet, use Google or use their Apps on their iPads. They subscribe to e-Newsletters and product notifications from the various businesses that interest them and GIVES VALUE.

It is the best time in human history to be a consumer!!! Choice – on demand.

So, what if the ways of traditional marketers have become less effective? What if the cheese has moved? Just how can retailers reach their customers?

Through permission based, relationship marketing – namely email and search.

When I say permission based marketing I really mean – permission to build relationships together. Trust, holding hands and demonstrating the value between you and your beloved customers are vital to long term and committed relationships. If you can do this, like the Meatloaf song goes, they, "Will love you Forever"…Compare this with the old methods of loud and boisterous CLEARANCE SALES or GOB SALES…It was – whoever is the loudest, gets the most business…Not so much anymore…

Email and search are two top mediums for RELATIONSHIP MARKETING.

Relationship marketing means:

Asking your customers if they would like to receive communications. These communications or "campaigns" include:

- Time saving messages

- e-Newsletters or notifications that add value

- Insider specials events (preferred customer sales)

What does relationship marketing do?

It helps strengthen the link with your best customers though professional campaigns. These include follow ups such as Thank you for Shopping, Thank you for purchasing, Quote and open order, Delivery/service scheduling, Surveys, and Salesperson special occasion greetings. Also, you can use your data for targeting your customers by demographics and purchasing patterns, such as next and past purchase.

Relationship marketing is non-intrusive and non-abusive. It's not about a quick fix. It's about acknowledging your best customers (those that want to hear from you) and keeping them close by providing a tailored marketing approach.

It's is not a one size fits all. You can SEE what your customers like as far as promotions, products and information. Then you can give them more of what they want. You can do this because when you send them a campaign, you know what they click on (click-through).

For example, you could send a newsletter highlighting new product styles that you saw at a trade show. Then you could allow readers to click to find out more on each style. From the analytics you would see the most liked styles. This information from your customers before you invest in new merchandise would be – PRICELESS.

There is a ton more that you can do with relationship marketing - more that I could ever write about in one article. Here are 4 practices to follow when considering your relationship marketing strategy:

(1) Do it right, the first time

The proper way to develop any relationship is to commit to providing value. Think of your customers as people with families, jobs and homes. They are your brothers and sisters – not a warm body with a wallet. This is where I think the independents can beat the big boys.

Avoid the BATCH and BLAST. This approach sends the same message to everyone regardless of who they are, where they live and their history with you. Since people are not the same, customers eventually get upset and opt-out.

You can do better! You can do it right by sending smaller targeted communications with meaning. Learn how a database works and how to segment an audience based on some relevant criteria.

(2) Get your "crew" on board

When you watch the Olympics and see how the 8s row together, you see how teams work together. They are one in unison. They have a clear understanding of the objective and how to get there. The team that wins the gold has everyone pulling in the same direction. That can be your team!

You need to get all your people – your salespeople, your office people, your distribution people and your managers – trained properly in executing a relationship marketing program. That means showing them how it will improve their lives and make customers happier.

- Your salespeople can get more return customers, and thus increased SALES.

- Your delivery personal will not need to play telephone tag as much because they can send messages when a customer's order is ready.

- Your marketing people can develop faster campaigns that are much cheaper because it is all electronic. They can see the results of their work.

- Your managers can be sure that salespeople are following up and keeping in touch with customers. Individual targeted messages can be sent by administration but from the salespeople automatically.

(3) Build content with value in mind

Spammers - don't be one. Period.

Always think value and permission and you will avoid this trap. When sending any e-message, follow up or marketing campaign, ask yourself, *"Am I giving my customer value first?"* Then next ask, *"Is the campaign easy to read and quick to understand."*

When people read an internet ad this is what happens: They look at who it is from. If they know them and respect them they may open or click. If they are unsure, or do not need that service at this time, they delete or ignore. Then, they may look at the subject. If it grabs them, they may open or click. If not, they delete or ignore. If they choose to interact with it, they will scan it in about 6-10 seconds. If something grabs them, they will spend more time. If not, guess what? Delete or ignore.

Don't be surprised. The same thing happens with traditional marketing. The direct mail may get read or thrown away. The TV commercial may be fast forwarded. The radio station may get changed.

The beauty with relationship marketing is that you can actually track your results. Try your best to provide value, watch your open and click through rates and then improve...

(4) Learn from your successes and failures

Marketing has always been hit or miss. What I love about relationship marketing though is that it treats consumers with more respect. I believe that because you can more easily strive towards providing them with what they want because of the instant feedback.

If you give customers what they want – great service, great product, great value, you will get what you want – SALES.

If you try to get what you want – SALES – without learning what your customers want – you will not get SALES.

After each campaign monitor your customer's response and ask? How many people opened the message? What did they click on? Who forwarded it to a friend? How many opted out? What did they like? Did it produce any in-store leads?

How can you improve next time?

Whatever happens with your campaigns, if you seek to improve each time, you will develop better customer relationships. Your customers will stay with you and not go to your competition when they are in the market. That bond is your gold.

Relationship marketing through permission based and segmented digital campaigns can produce big results. The costs of this are miniscule in comparison to mailers to your existing customer base. Results will be better, if you engage in true permission marketing as the audience is warm. They have opted in. They said yes – contact me!

Nurture a customer list with relationship marketing – it could take your business to another level.

9. HARNESS THE POWER OF E-MARKETING

So, the consumer population is not growing that fast in all regions. Your baby boomer customers are retiring and have a fixed income. Your best customer's sons and daughters grew up with the internet and email. These new buyers are now becoming your best customers.

The key is to communicate in a new fashion to these baby boomers and their tech demanding children. They expect you to be a savvy marketer. That means that:

- They can find you on the internet easily.
- You give them a website experience that answers their questions, has a modern look and great functionality.
- You send them relevant information when you contact them.

Critical components with a smart e-Marketing system:

1. Customer Relations Management (CRM).
2. Precision Marketing.
3. Web based email publishing software

When these components are implemented properly, in unison, they produce maximum results and build better customer relations.

Customer Relations Management (CRM) software can be used to run daily business operations and manage your follow up. Whether you are using an EPR system (Enterprise Resource Planning), or a general small business package like QuickBooks, you should enter all your customer information. That includes all contact data and sales and purchase history. Some of these packages also record customer lead opportunities for future sales and possible next purchase.

Now, one of the beauties of a computer system is that it stores data in neatly organized tables in the background that you never see. Believe me, they exist. Well, it's time to do something smart with that data and those tables. It's time to "mine that gold!"

You do this with a precision instrument, not dynamite. Dynamite is pulling all your customers out of your database and grouping them in one big bucket. This is called blasting your customers. Some refer to it as an e-blast. This method should only be used for an e-Newsletter.

Precision marketing requires a precision instrument. This is what database segmentation does. It enables you to easily pick out parts of your customer database so more relevant campaigns and messages can be sent. Take a clothing store, for example. If you know your customers like a certain product line, say Nike, why not access that data when Nike announces a new collection and target market those customers?

Then, merge your data with a web-based email publishing software such as Constant Contact or Emma. You can send a personalized campaign.

Know this: the key element is your precision database segmentation. This is the vital link that allows your message to be read a greater percentage of the time.

Three Targeted Campaigns

The sky is the limit with e-Marketing campaigns but here are three favorites:

1. Opportunity follow-up.

2. Quote follow-up.

3. Next purchase follow-up.

Opportunity Follow-up: Opportunity follow up is done after a customer comes into your store – whether they came to buy or just to look. If they bought you get their email on check out. If they did not buy you get their email through a drawing or some sort of sign up. You can send an email to all those customers, thanking them for patronizing your store. You've started to build your relationships.

Also, ask your customer, "Would you like an email of your receipt?"

Quote Follow-up: Do you want to make more money with minimum effort? Simple – generate more quotes! In many businesses people don't buy on the first visit. However, if they come back, there is a very good chance they will buy. Whatever their reason is for not buying now, ask them to take a minute to get a quote before they leave. If their reason for not buying now is, "I need to talk to my spouse", or "I'm not sure about the color", or "I just don't know", or "I can't afford it", or "I want to shop around", or "it's too expensive", then a give a quote. Help your customer.

Always ask your customer, "Would you like an email of your quote?"

The key is: You get their info. Now you can FOLLOW UP! Call them and/or send a very relevant email or text.

Next Purchase Follow-up: Retailers who do this say that this technique accounts for up to 5% of their sales. As you are typing in the sale (or somewhere during the sales process) in front of the customer, just say, "This looks great. Is there anything else we can help you with in the future?"

Bingo – enter the info in your CRM. A triggered follow up can be sent.

Additional e-Marketing Tip: Track Results

One of the very cool things about e-marketing is that you can see the results of your efforts. Traditional media is tough to measure. It's almost impossible to determine how many people looked at your message and what they liked.

E-Marketing is traceable. You can see the results. Following are some e-Marketing metrics and what they mean:

• **Open rate** - the number of people who opened your campaign in a traceable way. Like all response numbers, open rates vary based on the quality of the database, the nature of the content, and level of segmentation. Very generally speaking, good lists should expect open rates of 20-30%. Good segmented campaigns commonly get over 50%.

• **Bounces** - emails that were kicked back as undeliverable by the receiving server or because of incorrect email addresses.

• **Click through** - the number of people who clicked at least one link in your campaign and what they clicked on. This shows what people are reading and what they liked about your email campaign.

• **Opt out** - the number of people who opted out of your email list. The lower, the better. Less than 1% is good. Over 3% could be an indication of poor content or over sending.

• **Forward** - the number of people who used your "send-to-a-friend" option or forwarded this campaign. This is how viral messages start.

Start innovating. Technology is about speed. Consumers expect contact that gives them relevant value, when they need it.

Many stores still do it ineffectively. NOW is the best time to get one up on your competition and distinguish yourself with your customers.

10. WHAT REALLY MATTERS!

How to succeed and prosper in an uncertain economy

I know. I know. I know. Sometimes volume is unpredictable. This is true for many businesses in the retail sector. I have been consulting in-the-field visiting an average of two stores per month for the past 15 years. And do you know what I see? Funny enough, there are always operations with exceptional profitability. There are always operations that are average. And, there are always those that are weak performers. In any economy, it is the same.

I believe that downturns are good.

They weed out the weak, and they make room for those committed people, those that are smart, hardworking and willing to adapt to change.

I'm straight up. Unless you are committed, hardworking and smart, or hire people who are, it is difficult to make it long-term in retail.

Now, those of you who are committed to long-term prosperity keep reading — this is about you!

As a business coach, it is wonderful working with retailers who are like you, because you are 100 percent committed to success and are willing to do what it takes, by making changes and choices, because you like new ideas.

One question I get is: "Why were sales targets missed?

The answer I give is: ***"We need to analyze your sales metrics!"*** Is it traffic, average sales or close ratio? Or, is it all three? That's where good retailers start. They don't panic or shrug and say, "Sales are down," and stop talking. They have concrete proof of why. Then, they fight!

You need to know your metrics: daily, weekly, monthly, quarterly and year-to-date. In doing his you are able to spot downturns quickly and make changes to your operation faster.

Now, I'm sure you are all saying, "It is often just traffic— I know it!"

Ok, then, I'll focus on traffic. So, your traffic has been trending down— what can you do in the immediate future to offset that metric so that cash flow is healthy?

Well, I see many operations spending more cash on advertising and holding big promotions that cut into margins. If they just pump the well a little more — some water will still come up, right? No! If everyone is pumping the same well, the same way, what will the results be? Less water for everyone, of course!

Find a new well or a new way to drill it!

It's like the cheese in Spencer Johnson's best-selling tale, Who Moved My Cheese. The mouse that stayed and did the same "ole thing" by waiting, while the cheese got smaller, starved. The mouse that ***saw*** the cheese getting smaller, did something. He went hunting for cheese. Guess what? He got fat!

So if there is less water in the well, at the moment... less cheese, at the moment. There is less cash flow being generated, at the moment.

You are getting thirsty. Where should you look for water? Where do you find more cash?

Looking Inside Your Business

First, look within. This is the tough part for many so try to take emotion out of the equation. If your sales have reset down to a new level, your other operating costs must follow suit, as quickly as possible.

Cash, without changing debt, is really only produced from net income on the P&L (Profit and Loss Statement) and a reducing inventory. Improve these components and you will increase cash:

Gross Margin

If sales decline, average GM is often not enough to cover the fixed costs so that enough profit is produced.

Massive promotions that cut margin even more produce a negative cash flow. Margins need to go up, not down, to prosper.

• Concentrate on purchasing only best sellers for stock as they produce the highest ROI.

• Never repurchase slow selling, or non-proven items.

• Start pricing of new items at a higher GM percent margin for new items.

• Only discount slow moving items. Never discount best sellers, new items or special orders.

• Special orders are an opportunity for higher gross margin. Grab it every time! And, ask for payment, up front.

• Promote protection and warranty value every step of the way.

• Discount in steps according to the age of inventory so that turns and margin are maximized.

• Implement a variable commission for salespeople that is based on improved GM percent performance. The higher the GM sale, the higher the commission and vice versa.

Distribution

Many retailers are burdened with warehouse and shipping/delivery expenses. To increase cash flow via this area, you must be efficient in turning inventory fast.

• Make sure that all available merchandise in the warehouse is displayed each day.

• Schedule out-going freight fast.

• Use a routing and mapping technology, with GPS, to minimize fuel and time costs.

• Determine how many delivery crews are necessary to be delivering full trucks at all times.

• Set delivery charges at a rate so that all driving related costs, at least, are covered.

• Determine how much warehouse space is truly necessary for your ideal inventory level. Get rid of or sub-lease extra storage.

• As an alternative, explore hiring out delivery, but not warehousing.

Service

Any time there is a service issue on an item, the true profit of that sale is lost. This alone can be the difference between a profit or loss for the year. Declare war on operational mistakes, damages and defects. To accomplish this:

• Verify product design specs multiple times with the customer, salesperson and vendor on all special and custom orders. Follow-up and acknowledge often.

• Then, on all deliveries and customer pick-ups, prepare, deluxe and closely inspect all items, without exception.

• If there are any blatant vendor damages or imperfections, take a picture, and document the work to repair it and seek vendor credit for the expenses.

• Load and pack professionally and have the drivers take responsibility for the integrity of the product.

• Always apologize for issues and make it right with the customer. Word of mouth powerful.

This will not eliminate all problems of course, but it will greatly reduce the amount of customer service issues, increase credits and save many sales. There is a lot of extra business produced when customers are happy.

Sales Department

Salespeople need to be managed. Management needs to provide proper ongoing training in your selling processes. After this the salespeople and sales team should be measured not only on total sales but on its components:

Sales = Average Sale x Close Rate x Traffic

Average performers should be trained, motivated and elevated.

Weak performers should be removed and replaced, fast, preferably within the trial employment period.

Top performers, you can let run, provided they are team players. No top performer is worth keeping if they poison the team.

• Define your selling process.

• Determine the proper number of salespeople for your traffic. This number may differ depending on selling process. For example, a store that is traffic and immediate sale focused will require a higher traffic per salesperson than a store that is lifestyle focused.

- Track your metrics.

- Focus on team building and improvement.

- Eliminate weakness, poor attitudes, and constraints, fast.

- Don't be understaffed and never be overstaffed with the wrong people.

Administrative Costs

This is often a hard part of your business to "look within". Let's focus on you, as the Owner, GM or CEO. Temporally take emotion out of the equation. Add up all the salary, bonus, rent, meals and any non-critical business related expenses that run through your company. That total should only be paid if there is a profit. Loss is not an option.

Those businesses that take money out even if there is a loss, for whatever reason, force loans and eventually they run their wells dry. Selling of any fixed asset types is their final step. Don't go there. Pay yourself appropriately — from profit.

With employees, embrace the practice of rewarding fewer administrative people better. A great employee with a great attitude is worth three average employees in my book and 10 sub-par performers with poor attitudes are worth nothing. Creating a career for the great people in your business is vital to long-term success. Remove weakness and poor attitudes, immediately.

There are many other administrative associated costs — just ask yourself with each one, "How does this help my business?"

Inventory

You sell inventory and services. Here are some keys to tapping into a lucrative inventory well:

- Carry the appropriate amount of inventory for your sales volume and product segment.

- If you are over inventoried, stop buying NEW merchandise. Continue to buy proven items and special orders.

- Start buying new merchandise again, when your inventory to sales level has been corrected.

- Identify and mark down slow turning items fast and in successive steps. Do not rely on a semi-annual clearance sale as the sole strategy to move merchandise.

- GMROI is critical (Gross Margin Return on Investment is discussed in detail in the Inventory section). Know the GMROI of categories and vendors. Correct areas of weaknesses. Expand areas of strength.

Looking Outside Your Business

After taking a hard look at your business within, next look outside. What can you do better to bring customers in? They are out there somewhere and still spending money. They just may be spending money somewhere else, or saving, or paying debt. How can you reach out to them? Or, how can you make more from those that you do reach?

Advertising and Marketing Strategy

Recently, I was in a business which cut advertising by 25%. Guess what happened? Sales did not decline. They did this through shifting out of traditional medias of advertising such as newspaper, yellow pages and radio. They invested it into digital marketing medias such as email, Google and Facebook paid ads. With traditional advertising, if you can prove to yourself that a certain media is producing a good ROI, use it. Otherwise don't bother trying to do a little of everything ineffectively. If you have no proof, try something new.

Selling Strategy

You need a defined selling system. It should outline the ways in which your salespeople can help increase your average sales, close rate, and traffic. Focus more on your customer's lifestyles and desires and less on single items. Require each salesperson to follow your system where you have laid out the process from first contact through service after the sale. If you have a good system in place your average sales will increase along with your close rate.

You can increase traffic by better follow up with those customers who don't buy on first contact. This can be done through a variety of media. It really depends on how the individual customer wishes to be contacted. It could be text, a phone call at work, on their cell phone, Facebook message, direct tweet, Skype, Facetime or email.

There are so many ways to improve the production of "your well" or find "more cheese". There always will be. Just look for new and creative methods. Innovate. Talk to people who can help you improve. Smart businesses are the ones that prosper in all types of situations. This is the time of opportunity!

11. PAY FOR PERFORMANCE

"My bottom line is 15%." That was what a member in one of my performance groups modestly reported. "Wow!" and "How?" That was the reaction from the audience.

In a time when businesses with average profitability were reporting around 5% net income, this company was at the top of its game. Were they just lucky? Were they an anomaly? I think not. I've seen similar break out performances many times.

It comes down to this: to win you must create a business environment that breeds success – everywhere.

You see, a prime reason, why top performing companies outperform their average performing peers, is they pay extra when their people achieve better results. These successful businesses align their self-interests with their employee's self-interests. They have a well-executed Pay for Performance strategy (PFP). They understand that everyone deserves to make money – especially when they make the business money.

In this writing I will go over how to create a winning PFP strategy for your retail business.

The goal with PFP is to reward performance on the upside, above normal performance levels. This is not intended to replace your regular salaries or bread and butter sales commissions. It is intended to focus people's attention on helping you accomplish certain business objectives. PFP costs you nothing if executed correctly since you only pay when productivity is increased. Best of all, it gives people a vested interest in your success by focusing their attention on your organizational goals.

There are five basic steps to implementing a winning PFP strategy:

Step #1 - Set Performance Objectives

"I don't care how much power, brilliance or energy you have, if you don't harness it and focus it on a specific target, and hold it there you're never going to accomplish as much as your ability warrants." ~ Zig Ziglar.

Goals and micro-goals are the basis for PFP. You must know specifically where you need improvement to establish proper goals. Furthermore, you must know specifically how to make that improvement. For example, suppose you realize that your warranty close rate averages 10% on sales that can have product warrantees. Knowing that the best performing operations can close over 90%, it tells you that this is an area of opportunity. You can set a performance objective to improve warranty sales. If you achieve this micro-goal, your bigger goals of increasing sales and gross margin could also be realized.

Step #2 - Determine the Payment

Once you have your target set, you need to define the motivating element. Choose the "carrot" for the "rabbits" to chase. This should be customized to your situation and your people. It could be money, paid time off, merchandise, dinner vouchers, sports' tickets; you name it. Don't be afraid to be creative and fun. Let's say that you interview your sales associates and find that cash should be the "carrot". And just for fun, let's make this a team PFP program. After working the numbers, you decide to pay $1,000 per quarter to all sales associates for a 10% increase in the warranty close rate over the previous quarter's close rate.

Step #3 - Define How It Works

Keep it simple. Have the performance metric and term of measurement clearly defined whether it be a weekend, a month, a quarter, or a year. Have the people that are responsible for performing, track and measure the metric that you are trying to improve every week. This will keep you moving toward your target. They will learn more about effecting their performance if they measure it. By measuring along the way, you can see if changes in strategy, methods, or further education are needed. When it comes time to assess the final performance, you will already know if you have obtained the result that you were seeking.

Continuing the example, if a close rate of 20% is reached on warranty sales at the end of the quarter, the team gets to split $1,000. This is all up side, for everyone. There is no loss to the business. Everyone is happy. The salespeople make more, you make more, and the customer gets a value-added service. If the PFP program did not work, try again next quarter or make a change to the program.

Step #4 - Add, Drop, Change, Replace

Like merchandise, like employees, like vendors, like all things, some PFP programs will work better than others. If you create one that everyone likes, performance clearly improves and it is it easy to manage - You've got a winner. Let your winners run. Keep them on-going. On the other hand, if you have a PFP program that is not producing the desired results, tweak it if the metric is worth the effort to improve. However, don't be afraid to drop and replace programs to change the focus of your goals as your organization changes.

Let's say that you get your warranty close rates up to 70% on a consistent basis and you are happy with that. The effort that it might take to get it up to 90% might not be worth the time. Instead, you may decide to discontinue that program and replace it with a PFP program that focuses on increasing average sales per individual. Keep your PFP strategy dynamic.

Step #5 - Set the Rules

Think of it as a game. Be creative. Keep it simple. Keep it fun. Let others keep score. Results are reported to you – pay when your goals are realized. Cheaters are dismissed.

One important aspect to understand when creating your PFP strategy is that ALL departments and business partners should be considered for inclusion. Try not to leave anyone out. Improving sales metrics is not the only factor that contributes to increased cash flow and profitability. Any function worth improving should be considered. All departments: Sales, Marketing, Customer Service, Warehouse, Accounting, and of course Management. You can even consider developing PFP for external partners such as vendors and your best customers to communicate your appreciation.

(The following 2 pages contain program examples only. You should adapt these to fit your type of business and compensation structure.)

Pay for Performance Example

Job Function	Performance Objective	Payment	How it works
Sales Associates	Increase turns and free up cash by selling slow moving or excess inventory faster.	Spiff markdown items or groups to draw attention to merchandise that is being dropped. Varies on age of item: $10-$100 per item or group.	Selectively choose items on your mark down report where you wish to add an extra bonus. Print a spiff list once per week for spiff items available. Periodically change the items being spiffed to keep it fresh.
Sales Team	Exceed monthly written and delivered volume goals.	1 free vacation day / salesperson	If both written and delivered sales surpass targets, the sales team gets an extra vacation day.
Sales Manager	Increase core sales metrics: average sale x close rate x # of ups	$1000 in store voucher for every increase in all 3 metrics / quarter.	Track using a salesperson effectiveness report that details: Written sales, # of selling opportunities (ups or traffic), Average Sale, Close ratio, Revenue per up (PIN #), Gross Margin.
Combined PFP: Sales Manager and Inventory Manager	Keep inventory to sales ratio within responsible range. Get 2 key positions working together.	Car allowance.	For every quarter that the inventory to sales ratio stays between 14-18% a car allowance of $500 for both the sales manager and the buyer will be extended for the next quarter.
Buyer or Inventory Manager	Increase GMROI.	For every 10 cent improvement in GMROI over quarterly average, pay a % of value.	A 10 cent improvement at $1,000,000 in inventory is $100,000 in extra GM / year; if you pay 2% / quarter that is a $2,000 bonus.
Administrator	Obtain rewards from using company credit cards responsibly.	% of Vacation award points or % of cash back.	Many credit cards give a spiff for usage. Have your administrator find the most beneficial card for your particular business. Bonus from a % of the award. The credit card must be paid off in full each month and 0 interest should be incurred.
Head Book keeper or Controller	On time and accurate monthly reporting.	1 dinner for 2. Per quarter at any restaurant.	If all financial and other required reporting are accurate and submitted by the 10th of each month without fail, the reward is given.
Controller	Increase cash flow by increasing Current and Quick Ratio targets.	$1000 at year end for achieving goals.	Establish a quick and current ratio target for cash flow using a pro forma (budgeted) financial statement. Track and report each month to management team.
Warehouse	Maintain a 100% accurate inventory.	Movie vouchers.	Weekly, the controller picks a random location. If there are 0 exceptions the prize is awarded.

Job Function	Performance Objective	Payment	How it works
Delivery / Shipping Scheduling	Increase speed of delivery scheduling. Maximize utilization of truck space.	$100 / week when over 95% of completed sales are scheduled.	Review a sales complete for delivery report on a weekly basis to determine metric and bonus.
Drivers	Perfect deliveries (No damages).	Pick a discontinued piece of merchandise (under retail $1000).	All deliveries are delivered to the customer's in perfect order. Must not have any refusals or service issues for the month.
Service	Decrease service as a % of delivered sales.	Tickets to NHL hockey game.	Determine areas of issues each month. Figure # of items with service / delivered sales x 100. Issue prize on decrease.
Distribution Manager	Keep controllable warehouse expenses under the budgeted level.	Split a proportion of expenses that are under targeted levels on the budget-$ and % of sales.	When controllable expense are under targeted dollar and % of sales levels split them by a predetermined proportion.
IT (Info Tech)	Achieve a 100% up time of all critical systems.	Internal tech: $100 best buy gift cards; External: Negotiate a rate structure.	Controller tracks down time per month during operating hours.
Marketing? That's Everyone!	Increase traffic through word of mouth.	Spilt commission for any employee referrals.	Get cards made up for everyone in your company. If a customer comes in and gives the card to a salesperson the commission will be split.
Total team, customers and a charity organization	Total team building and reinforcing PFP program.	Recognize 1 person for above and beyond performance. $500 to charity of winners choice / month	Employees and Customers can vote for an employee. Have a Charity Box and online form that says "Tell us if an employee went above and beyond."
All employees and managers	Promote a healthy lifestyle and tie it into the performance of the business.	Annual Company Fitness Membership (1st yr free).	Must meet or exceed profitability and cash flow targets.
General Management / Ownership	Increase company profitability and cash flow to enable long term survival and maximize shareholder EPS (Earnings per share).	% of profitability that exceeds pro forma target for profitability. Both cash flow and profitability targets must be met.	Annual bonus based on financial performance of the entire business. Note: The financial statements must be certifiably correct. They should also by normalized due to shareholder withdrawals, for example.
Your Big Customer's	Create buzz around town amongst your biggest customers and their friends.	Super Bowl Tickets. Or, a 1 week trip to Aruba.	The customer with the most purchases gets a super bowl weekend or a trip to Aruba. Invite 100 finalists to a private party to announce the winner.

INVENTORY

12. DYNAMIC INVENTORY MANAGEMENT

One of the biggest challenges and opportunities of today's retailers is with inventory management. Poor inventory practices are common in many operations. The result is a cash flow drain rather than a cash flow gain.

In this writing I will discuss ways in which you can measure and then improve the health of your inventory. It doesn't matter if you are an independent, a branded store or a big box; your return on inventory determines the velocity of your cash flow. The faster you turn your merchandise and the higher the margin you turn it at, the faster you will accumulate cash. Retailers who focus primarily on maximizing sales volume will produce average results. High profit companies place equal focus on the quality of their inventory. If you can execute inventory management practices that are better than your competitors, you will outperform them in both profit and cash flow at an equal sales volume.

The first step to take to maximize cash flow with inventory management is to:

Check your metrics often. If you skip this step, you cannot possibly know where to apply your talent and business resources to maintain your inventory mix at optimal levels. Once you have a true picture of the quality of your inventory, and compare it with internal or external benchmarks, you will be aware of your strengths and weaknesses. Only then will you be able to set realistic goals for improvement, and then take action. Here are some key metrics that you should calculate:

GMROI: Increasing gross margin return on inventory (GMROI) should be a primary business objective. <u>The higher your GMROI, the faster your cash flow velocity.</u> It measures how many gross margin dollars you produce per dollar of inventory invested.

GMROI = annual gross margin dollars / inventory on hand.

Use average inventory numbers if you have them, but keep the time-frame shorter than three months, so that you can gauge improvement. Gross margin dollars are calculated by deducting average landed cost of goods sold from sales. You should annualize the actual or projected gross margin.

Let's say an operation carried an average inventory at a cost of $3,300,000 and had annual sales of $20,000,000 at a 45% gross margin.

GMROI = ($20,000,000 x 45%) / $3,300,000 = $2.72 GMROI.

There is a big difference in a few cents too. For example, if one operation produced a GMROI of $2.72 while another operation produced a GMROI of $2.5. The difference of $0.22 translates into $220,000 per year in gross margin per million dollars in inventory!

Inventory to sales ratio: This ratio serves as a quick gauge of whether or not you are over-inventoried for your projected sales volume. Measure this ratio by dividing inventory on hand by annual sales. In home goods retail, for example, most profitable companies maintain a ratio of between 15 to 17%. Other faster ordering product industries may be as low as 6%.

Whatever your efficiency range, inventory to sales is a useful indicator when looking at purchasing new product. A good rule of thumb is to buy only best sellers and special order items if you are over your target level. Avoid purchasing new untested product if you are running an inventory to sales ratio higher than your goal. Your inventory number typically includes all reserved, damaged and display only items (aka nail-downs). Sales are annualized or realistically projected.

Sales per square foot: This metric measures the efficiency of your showroom. It shows you where you can be for your current size and type of business. I typically see stores running between $200 – $500 sales/square feet. Oh, the leader in retail sales per square foot is Apple at over $6000!

Best seller in-stock days: The well-established 80/20 rule of retail says that the top 20% of your items generate 80% of your gross margin dollars. The bottom 80% produce only 20% of your gross margin dollars, with many items producing $0. Items that fall within your top 20% are your best sellers while those in the bottom 80% that produce $0 are your dogs. Once you have identified the top 20% of your items, see how often they are in stock. The best stores have their best sellers in stock 95%+ of the time. The greater the amount of time you have your best items in stock and the fewer your stock-out days, the faster you will generate cash. Imagine if an Apple Store ran out of the iPhone in white – what would happen to sales?

Percentage of current inventory: This ratio tells you the percentage of your inventory that is current: meaning items that are either best sellers or new to the line-up.

Measure % of current inventory by adding the total number of top selling items in stock to the total number of new items (less than 60 days in inventory). Then, divide the total by the number of in stock inventory items overall.

The result is an indicator of whether or not you are effective in turning slow moving items fast to make room for new merchandise. Companies with a small proportion of their inventory that is current, tend not to be trying new items often enough. They are often clogged with slow or not selling items (dogs). They have not reacted quickly enough to rectify the situation. Well-run operations have a high percentage of current merchandise (commonly above 75%). They recognize and sell their dogs fast and they purchase new items to replace dogs, fast.

Merchandise to display percentage: You can only sell something if your customers and salespeople know about it. Some retailers can have substantial amounts of merchandise not on display. This can be due to slow moving warehouse distribution networks, over inventoried showrooms or just ignorance. Try to have 99% of available items on display, at any given time. The faster you identify and display these items, the greater your turns will be.

Percentage of sales orders complete for delivery and scheduled: The high majority of customers that can be shipped should be scheduled. You may find that you are slow to notify and schedule customers when their merchandise is ready. The best stores keep their customers informed through the entire process from initial greeting to after delivery. Track this metric so that you become more proactive in your efforts to notify and ship to your customers. Gross margin is only realized after delivery. You will produce greater cash flow, revenue and GMROI if you can reduce the amount of time reserved merchandise sits in the warehouse as work-in-process (WIP).

Check these metrics at least once a month so that you can spot problem areas. Then use management tactics to advance your company performance.

The Process of Dynamic Inventory Management

This diagram shows the general inventory life-cycle flow for best sellers and slow moving items:

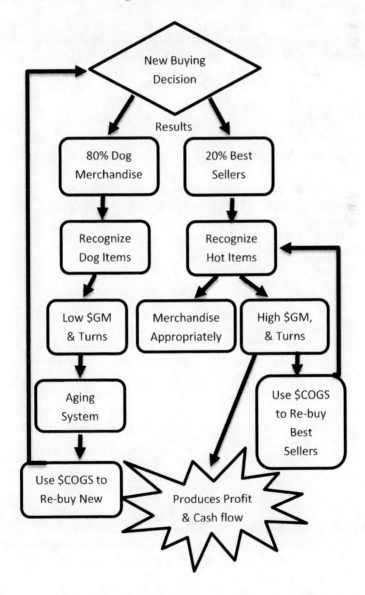

The process is driven by active recognition that approximately 20% of inventory items are your best sellers, and approximately 80% are also-rans and dogs. The usefulness of the chart is that it outlines a process for reinvesting your inventory dollars in a way that will maximize GMROI and cash flow.

Your margin dollars should go towards covering your operating costs and contribute to profit, while the cost of goods sold that you recover from the sale should be used to repurchase either hot items or new items. The sales proceeds from your best sellers should be used to repurchase best sellers at the correct time and in the correct quantities. With the eventual sale of dogs you should repurchase new items, only if you are at a proper inventory level (15% inventory to sales, for example). You should never re-buy a dog.

Be aware of the fact that your inventory is constantly changing, and eventually best sellers do become dogs. When you see that a best seller isn't selling anymore, act fast.

Best Sellers, Dogs & New Items

Even though best sellers will only represent 20% of your items, it is impossible to remember each one of them in their different product lifecycles. That's why you need to analyze and sort items monthly by gross margin written over the prior 3-6 months. Make sure that you have these items in stock, displayed properly, and on-order in the correct quantities.

Take steps to keep them in the forefront of your employee's minds. Salespeople should know which items are best-sellers and where they are located, because these are, typically, the easiest products to sell. Your buyers should continually track hot items. Warehouse and merchandise managers must take care to display them promptly in all relevant showrooms.

As well, you should analyze, in summary, the GMROI for each vendor and category. You can determine where your strengths and weaknesses with respect to other categories and vendors. Doing this on a monthly basis will help you to spot trends and measure the effectiveness of your inventory management strategy.

By spotting your best categories, vendors and items, you establish a re-purchasing priority. When you have this important information at your fingertips, you can buy from performing merchandise areas when needed.

Customers often want and expect immediate fulfillment of displayed items, so best sellers should be kept in-stock at appropriate quantities. Dogs can be sold off the floor any time, As-Is. New items are an exception with display. When you are testing a new item, it is appropriate to keep it "nailed" down.

Stock-outs of best sellers can be a major downside due to buying new items before re-buying hot items. Once you have identified your best sellers, look at these primary factors to consider when reordering:

•Rate of sale over the prior six months.

•Available in-stock and available on-order.

•Reorder lead-time.

•Reorder minimum.

Commonly, buyers meet with reps and make decisions based on factory data and intuition. This is generally not a good idea. All purchases should be backed up by your data – not someone else's information or a "gut feeling". Factory data typically does not contain detailed retail selling information. Your suppliers cannot properly identify your best sellers by GMROI. Neither can they tell you the correct time to re-purchase.

Flushing Dogs

Equally important as spotting hot items and purchasing them, is identifying your slow moving items so that you can flush them out of your line-up sooner.

Tracking dog merchandise is even more challenging than tracking winners. Winners almost take care of themselves because everyone loves them – or should. Dogs however are commonly ignored. They clog up your showroom and take extra warehouse space. They strangle your profit and cash flow by limiting your ability to re-purchase new items that may have become best sellers. They force your organization into stagnation. They create merchandise flow bottlenecks.

To get out of this retail trap, or break the bottleneck, implement an inventory aging system. As mentioned before, a fast turning store will have over 75% of their inventory value current (new items less than 60 days old and best sellers). To get started, set six aging periods on your merchandise categories where each period is 60 days long.

This is a step approach to inventory reduction. It allows you to maximize GMROI by recognizing and taking action on dogs faster than a semi-annual clearance sale, for example. Here you will gain in both turns and gross margin.

When companies age their inventory out every 60 days for the first time, many are shocked by the realization of how old their inventory really is. Current inventory may be so low that the system is unworkable due to the large number of old items requiring immediate attention. If this is your experience, set your aging dates out far enough to produce around a 75% current inventory. This allows for a more manageable start to the system.

At each aging period, identify dogs and take specific actions. These actions can range from simply marking them down by 10% per period, to taking steps such as re-merchandising, spiffing salespeople, un-nailing display, packaging, advertising, and moving items to clearance centers.

Regardless of the actions you take to solve the ongoing dog challenge, your goal should be to <u>identify non-selling items and *do something*</u> so that you don't succumb to merchandise stagnation.

Each month, execute your aging system. As your current aging increases, shorten your aging days to turn inventory faster.

If you flush out your dogs, while purchasing new items at the correct time, you will sustain a profitable level of inventory. After you achieve this, leverage your systems for new merchandise buying.

New Buying

So, when should you buy new merchandise and how much should you buy?

Once you have all your best sellers on order, you should try new untested items if you are under your target inventory to sales ratio. Suppose that ratio is 15% for your type of retail business. If you consistently operate at that level typically you will more often have the cash to try new merchandise.

Dollars for purchasing new items come from the cost of selling items that did not work out. Any margin eventually made on these old items ideally can go towards operating costs, while the cost (COGS) can ideally go toward buying new merchandise.

For example, if your company has a desired inventory to sales ratio of 15% and you find that you are below this level, start tracking the cost of your dogs sold through your inventory aging system. Put this value either on a spreadsheet or into a real bank account. Make these funds available for "open to buy new".

When you go to trade shows or meet with reps, you will know how much you have available to spend. Following this practice, you will not become over inventoried provided that your sales are constant. If you use more funds than are available, you will eventually lose cash flow due to the odds of the 80/20 rule of retail that says that 80% of your new purchases will be also-rans and dogs; only 20% will become best sellers.

A word of caution: don't fall into the trap of buying new in anticipation of selling your dogs within the product lead time. This practice almost never works, and a shortage of cash will be the likely result.

Once you know how many dollars you have in your "open to buy new account", you will need a system to help you find which new products you should buy.

If, for example, you have $20,000 in an open to buy fund, you should look to areas that are currently performing with an above average GMROI. The best way to do this is rank your vendors under each category by gross margin dollars and look at the GMROI of each vendor.

Invest in your highest producing areas. If one category has a high GMROI compared to your industry high profit standards and compared with your other categories, this high GMROI category would be a good candidate for new investment.

Once you've identified the top categories, take a look at your vendor rankings within each category. You will most likely have one or two vendors that are out-performing all others in GMROI.

Finally, look at your current lineup with respect to your price points displayed to see if you are sufficiently covered. Put your money in areas of strength and watch the numbers closely after the merchandise arrives.

After making the decision to purchase new products, you need to closely follow their dynamic product lifecycle. New merchandise is for testing. The objective is to put the product in front of your customers to gauge their response. If they like a new style, it will become a best seller in your ranking system. If not, it will show up as a dog in your inventory aging system.

Even if your new product is a potential winner, it is still necessary to treat new items properly to maximize your GMROI. Don't buy new products and forget to look after them. Follow these important operational steps to ensure the proper testing of your new items:

•PO Follow-up – Acknowledge all POs, without exception. Verify your orders, check costs and determine ETA dates. Your purchasing clerk should produce a non-acknowledged report weekly to see what is falling through the cracks.

•100% Inventory Accuracy – Control over this asset is a requisite for its management. If you carry inventory, you should be bar coding. Otherwise you cannot fully benefit from inventory management due to the high probability of error in quantities and locations. Receiving needs to be immediate and locations exact – period.

•Fast Display – Your merchandiser and buyers should display new merchandise within 1-2 days of its arrival. Routinely, access merchandise that is available to be displayed. This will improve your speed of sales.

•Proper Pricing – Once your merchandise arrives and the actual landed costs are calculated, your buyer should physically look at the product and price within the proper price point. By doing this you will gain additional gross margin.

•Nail down – Your merchandiser and sales manager should ensure that new items will not be sold from display during an initial test period (usually 60 days). Unless you are a cash and carry type of retailer, the floor model can be used to create customer orders or sell from back-up stock.

•Proper Display – Display and accessorize in a high traffic area to maximize customer exposure.

•Sales Training – Your sales manager and reps should train your employees on the features and benefits of each new group.

•Tracking & Analysis – Have sales manager and buyers keep track of new items systematically and discuss results at least each month.

•Fast Shipping – Your delivery scheduler needs to schedule in stock items for fast delivery. Make sure that you get and review reports of sales that are fully deliverable.

•Don't Forget Proper Accounting – Many companies do not accurately cost their merchandise. It is imperative that your office manager check your invoice cost against your receiving cost and adjust where necessary to make sure that you have the correct information for your decision making.

Managing Inventory Change

Daily operational excellence with dynamic inventory management will maximize your cash flow in the long run provided that you are committed to managing the process.

Following-up with the right people is a key to successful execution. Inventory management is about managing changes in the merchandise lifecycle. Several individuals in your organization need to be intimately involved in the process.

•Follow-up often!

•Continuously review the inventory lifecycle process.

•Develop a task list that specifies each task, the team member responsible and the objectives and measurement to be taken.

Finally, *inspect what you expect!* Have weekly operations meetings with your team and require them to report on their performance. Have the metrics, reports and data to back it up. If people are missing their targets, identify issues and find a solution — fast. Your employees will know what is expected of them and see their performance as being a critical part of your company's success.

Everyone will benefit from improving your dynamic inventory management process. Your customers will get more selection, more available items, greater value and faster service. Your employees will get a more rewarding work atmosphere, better day to day procedures, a faster turning floor, and a more secure company to work for. As an owner you will see your company generate cash and profit faster and you will be able to compete more effectively in today's tough retail environment.

"Dogs Tend to Sit!" ~ Vela

13. THE BUYER

A buyer's job does not end with the filing of a purchase order.

Buyers should be your most important inventory managers. They control the tap that determines merchandise flow. Inventory flow has the greatest impact on cash flow because it makes up the largest proportion of assets for many retailers. It is, therefore, critical that all buyers become expert inventory managers and that their duties do not end at the time when they send a purchase order.

Buyers, who are directly involved in the inventory management process, produce a higher return on their inventory. This is the result of the production of greater Gross Margin dollars and also faster turns. Gross Margin is greater in part because these buyers set pricing levels that account for "perceived product values" with the goal of selling at ideal price points.

Alternatively, a buyer who adds new merchandise too quickly, adversely effects turns and Gross Margin percent. That is because this practice invariably results in large, clearance sales to move excess inventory. Turns are slower because older, unpopular merchandise tends to sit in stock longer than it should.

Focusing on purchasing only, causes a company to become over inventoried and experience cash shortages. If purchases of new merchandise are made prior to selling the old merchandise, non-performing items (dogs) accumulate. In turn, assets yield a tradeoff of cash for inventory.

Systems define outcomes.

Buyers can only become true inventory managers, maximizing GMROI and cash flow, when they work closely with the following key aspects of an inventory lifecycle system:

• The Purchase Order

• Purchase Order follow-up

• Receiving

• Display of merchandise

• Sales Analytics & Performance Tracking

The Purchase Order

It is the buyer's responsibility to make sure that all item orders are created properly, and categorized appropriately. The buyer should also double check to make sure that costs are correctly noted to allow for the best inventory analysis later on. Buyers should send Purchase Orders to the vendor representative and reference the correct internal system Purchase Order number, not vice versa.

Operations where Purchase Orders are made by vendor representatives usually experience procedural breakdowns due to Purchase Orders not being entered properly in the retailer's inventory tracking system. Companies are improving on the vendor communication process through EDI (electronic data interchange), email or web interface.

Purchase Order Follow-up

Next, the head buyer should oversee the follow-up process. Once a Purchase Order is sent, the vendor should acknowledge your order.

If they don't do this, require that they do so. A purchase order confirmation allows you to check the accuracy of items ordered, quantities and costs. It also gives an estimated ship date so that all employees can speak intelligently to customers on special orders about when their product might be available for delivery. By entering realistic arrival information into your system, salespeople can more easily follow-up with both vendors and customers when a shipment is overdue.

Receiving

Buyers who communicate well with distribution managers regarding expected receiving dates help the warehouse to efficiently receive inventory into the system. Bar code labels, sold lists, transfer lists, and restocked item lists can all be generated in advance. Good communications cut down on merchandise handling time and errors. The time inventory is in the warehouse can be kept to a minimum.

Display

Buyers should also be responsible for working with Merchandisers to create immediate merchandise transfer orders. This gets available to sell merchandise in the showroom sooner. Buyers and Merchandisers together should take time to physically look at the product arrivals to establish proper pricing. This interaction between buyers and merchandisers helps to accurately establish which items can fetch a higher retail price and which items must be priced lower for competitive reasons. Operations that have this personal approach to pricing and displaying of merchandise maximize their margin opportunity. These operations also remain competitive and experience fewer gaps in price points because they take existing showroom line-ups into account.

Sales

Great buyers work with sales managers to identify both best sellers and dog inventory on a routine basis. This team approach is the key to turning merchandise faster and keeping the best mix on the floor.

Once identified, popular items can be re-ordered at the appropriate time and quantity to ensure "just in time" inventory. Stores that take this approach have higher sales, because the best sellers are in stock a greater percentage of time. These stores also take action sooner to move out slow movers. Once slow moving items are sold, new merchandise can be tested. Great buyers do not wait until clearance sales.

Sales Analytics & Performance Tracking

Improvement starts with measuring performance. Exceptional buyers seek to improve return on investment produced by the various vendors and categories. They analyze each of them on a monthly basis and track sales, cost, merchandise in stock, on order, Gross Margin, turns, price points displayed, best seller in stock days, and most importantly GMROI. Vendors and categories that are under performing are focused on. Constant improvements are sought. Vendors that improve and produce are embraced and expanded while those that do not improve are phased out. Emotion and loyalty should not eclipse the trends and numbers.

Prior to purchasing new merchandise, analytics should be used to determine when the inventory flow tap for purchasing new products needs to be turned on or off. When inventory is too great for the current sales level, good buyers do not purchase untried new products. If inventory is at a favorable level to sales, then new buying commences at the proper level and time. In this way buyers do not strain cash flow. They contribute to cash flow!

Use the following job description to assist in the development of your most important inventory manager, your head buyer:

Head Buyer / Inventory Manager
Inventory Management Co-coordinator

The following statements are intended to describe the general nature and level of work being performed. They are not intended to be construed as an exhaustive list of all responsibilities, duties, and skills required of personnel so classified.

SUMMARY

The Head Buyer / Inventory Manager will ensure that special order merchandise is correctly ordered, stock merchandise is replenished in accordance with approved guidelines, on order merchandise is tracked and inventory excesses are eliminated. Analysis and reports will be sent to management on all aspects of purchasing / inventory management functions.

DUTIES AND RESPONSIBILITIES

- On a daily basis, reviews all system generated purchase orders of special order merchandise, ensures that the correct merchandise order is being placed, and checks both stock and open stock purchase orders for availability of the identical merchandise.
- Generates purchasing reports for the replenishment of regular stock merchandise.
- Reviews purchasing reports and creates stock purchase orders, based on a pre-determined schedule for each applicable vendor.
- Ensures that purchase order acknowledgements are reviewed and entered in the system daily and that all costs and arrival times are confirmed and updated.
- Follows up with vendors on the status of all open purchase orders, including those which are non-acknowledged or those which are late in arrival.
- On a monthly basis, runs the system generated inventory aging report to identify and price inactive inventory.
- Maintains the complete inventory aging system to efficiently and economically move the inventory dogs.

- Produces sales analysis reports to identify best sellers and communicate with the sales manager.
- Tracks performance of vendors and categories.
- Implements strategies to improve GMROI.
- Maintains merchandise to be displayed system.
- Maintains an open to buy for new merchandise.
- Coordinates transfers and pricing with Merchandisers.
- Evaluates and works to improve vendor and category performance.
- Works closely with various departments.
- Meets with Vendor Reps to consider reorders, new orders and service issues.
- Attends trade shows to develop relationships.
- Performs miscellaneous job-related duties as assigned.

REQUIRED KNOWLEDGE, SKILLS, AND ABILITIES

Ability to co-ordinate with and train staff, including organizing, prioritizing, and scheduling work assignments.

- Great team building attitude.
- Records maintenance skills.
- Knowledge of retail and inventory management standards and procedures.
- Knowledge of purchasing practices in a retail environment.
- Ability to operate a computerized business management systems.
- Strong communication and interpersonal skills.
- Ability to gather data, compile information, and prepare reports.
- Ability to analyze and solve problems.

14. THE WEB OF EXCESS INVENTORY CONSEQUENCES

Using furniture retail as an example - this is why a high inventory relative to sales, slows sales, profits and cash flow.

Carrying too much inventory creates a host of web-like cost effects in your business. If you get caught in this web, it will slow down your business and result in a sticky situation that could be difficult to escape from. You could become immobilized, just like a fly staring into the eyes of a spider, waiting to get eaten.

You can escape this fate before you become too entangled, or avoid it altogether if you understand the reasons why so many companies get caught. Then you can evaluate your current situation, identify and untangle all of the effects that excess merchandise has on your sales, cash, and profitability.

The most profitable retail furniture operations in the world run their businesses continuously at around a 15% inventory to sales ratio (Average Inventory / Annual Sales). Some carry even less. This statistic has been published year after year by the NHFA (National Home Furnishings Association). It has been verified in my own consulting practice. It is important that you establish an inventory to sales target that makes sense for your specific retail segment. In home furnishings, there are no double digit profitability stores that carry over 20% inventory to sales for any extended period of time.

Why is it then that many home furnishings retailers run at much higher levels?

It is common to see stores over 20% and some at even over 30% inventory to sales levels. Owners and managers fail to take action, because they do not see inventory as a problem. Instead they see it as a solution, believing that they can buy themselves into profitability. Some say, "If we just buy the right merchandise, our sales will increase." Some say, "We are rich with all this inventory." They are usually short on cash flow, though.

Then, when sales stay the same or increase only slightly and the next furniture market rolls around, they say, "I think if we just try this new group; our sales will increase."

Yes, new buying is necessary, but it should only be done when inventory to sales levels are appropriately lean.

Another misguided practice is that retailers hang on to inventory as if it were an asset with a lot of liquidity. Although inventory is an asset, it is far from equal to cash. Cash, with prudent investment, appreciates with time and is liquid. Inventory depreciates and only best sellers are liquid. In fact, smart financiers don't even consider inventory when looking at the solvency of a business. They look at the quick ratio only. This is the ability to cover short term debt with current assets, excluding inventory.

Another reason why stores carry too much inventory is that they fail to react quickly when changing business conditions negatively impact their sales.

When the housing market slowdown hit in 2008, most dealers did not see it coming. They continued to buy at the same levels. Many reacted by making cuts in operating expenses when non best-selling inventory should have been cut first. The minority recognized the slowdown and reacted fast. These are the stores, which maintained high levels of cash flow and respectable profitability, even when sales declined.

Whether you are an independent store, branded, or a top 100 retailer, the benefits of managing inventory levels are too massive to ignore. Ask the Ashley Furniture Homestores! (I was actually involved in one of the first implementations). They now are bigger than Wal-Mart in this retail segment. **Lean inventory flow is at the heart of Ashley's massive success.** Similar to a mattress operation, Ashley stores commonly operate at 7-9% inventory to sales.

Maintaining similar efficiencies will be the primary factor in your long term survival as well as your ultimate success.

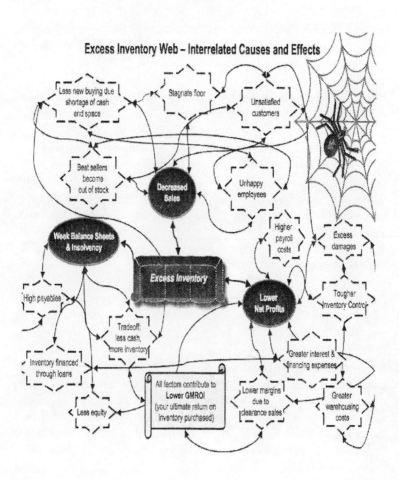

Excess Inventory Web – Interrelated Causes and Effects

Impact on cash, sales, and profit:

Getting caught in the excess inventory web has three big negative repercussions. It causes:

• A weak balance sheet, leading to insolvency.
• Lower sales.
• Smaller net profits.

Balance Sheet Impact

High inventory creates a weak balance sheet. I have seen that high profit companies have about 19% of assets in cash and 50% in inventory. Average stores have around 12% in cash and a much larger percentage in inventory dollars. Companies with too much inventory generally show increased liabilities on their balance sheets that are required to fund the larger payables. These companies require more short and long term loans.

The difference between a high profit and average operation with $10 million in total assets is about $700,000 in extra cash. Another way to look at this solvency effect is via inventory's relation to sales. An operation doing $10 million in sales running at 15% rather than 20% carries $500,000 less in inventory. Never forget: **CASH IS KING!**

Sales Impact

Excess inventory causes sales to drop. There are many factors that participate to create this affect. A major one is the increase in best seller out of stock days. High inventory ties up funds and reduces liquidity. As a result, fewer dollars are available to properly buy your best selling items. Since these items account for the majority of your revenue, when you run out...you lose. Nothing is more frustrating than not being able to order a container of your best selling goods because you have to make payroll or pay for your current payables due.

As well as not being able to purchase sufficient top merchandise, your floor will become stale, your existing merchandise will become old, and the showroom will become stagnant and clogged with dogs.

This causes a decline in another important measure: customer satisfaction. If you are not able to provide what your customers want, when they want it, they will stop buying and will adopt a negative perception of your brand. Worst of all, they will tell their family and friends. Your showroom will appear unfashionable and you will need to invest in higher levels of advertising to generate adequate traffic.

A stagnant floor also negatively affects the morale of your sales force. They, just like customers, love the latest and the greatest products. If you allow merchandise to sit, they will sit too. Sales motivation is the highest at fast moving, dynamic stores.

As a comparison, think of successful apparel retailers, like Banana Republic or Coach. They take action to recognize and get rid of old stock immediately. Competition is fierce, inventory is kept correct, customer service rules, and the best systems and procedures are implemented. The thought of being unstylish and old is not acceptable.

Profit Impact

Too much inventory results in a lower gross margin. If dogs are not recognized fast and moved out, they accumulate and overwhelm your systems. This is why many operations hold clearance sales, tent sales, and high-impact type promotions. Prices are slashed on a massive scale. GMROI suffers due to lower gross margin and slower turns. High profit and average stores are usually separated by three to five points in GM% for this reason.

Significant extra operating expenses are incurred as well. The following is a real example of the gain in profitability that was experienced by a store that decreased its' inventory to sales ratio from 25% to 15%:

- Gross Margin: +3%; eliminated excessive markdowns.
- Salaries: +1%; reduced extra people to receive, transfer, inventory control.
- Warehouse: +1%; reduced costs of equipment, supplies, maintenance.
- Customer Service: +.5%; reduced occurrence of damages.
- Occupancy Costs: +2%; eliminated unnecessary additional storage space.
- Interest Expense: +2%; reduced cost of loans needed to finance inventory and pay vendors.
- Net Income Effect: +9.5%

FYI: The most profitable operation that I have worked with produced a 10% inventory to sales. Their net income was 18%!

Unless you are an antique dealer, merchandise does not age like wine. It becomes more and more expensive to carry each day that it sits. Don't believe that if you hang on to a poor seller long enough, someone will buy it and you will get your margin out of it. Realize that this product takes up valuable floor space. Your GMROI will improve by embracing a strategy of turning items faster, replacing them with best sellers and new items sooner.

Whatever your retail segment, remember; don't stop buying your best sellers and special order merchandise. That is your lifeblood. Controlling new purchases, along with strategies to maximize turns and margin, will help you avoid and even escape the web of excess inventory consequences.

15. MARKDOWN STRATEGIES

Most retailers will agree that reducing the price of slow moving, discontinued, or seasonal merchandise will cause customers to eventually purchase these products. However, the process by which retailers execute their price markdown strategy to sell this dog merchandise can usually be improved.

First, dog merchandise is often identified too slowly. Some retailers only recognize an item if it does not sell in three to six months. By waiting this long, valuable floor space becomes stagnant and the opportunity cost of trying a different item in its place is missed.

Secondly, dog merchandise is sometimes not properly identified. Even if your store is small, you need an automated system to let you know which items are not moving. Retailers that rely on the feelings and memory of a trusted manager to supply this information, always miss items that should be marked down. They may even discount items that should not be marked down. Proper <u>systems tell the truth because they are unbiased</u>.

Lastly, dog merchandise is typically marked down too steeply. Many stores rely solely on big sales where prices are slashed. These are time consuming events that can be massive margin eaters. Sales are OK, but they should be conducted in accordance with an efficient markdown strategy whereby only the very oldest merchandise is sold at the largest discounts.

Measuring the Value of an Efficient Markdown System

An efficient markdown system has a considerable impact on profitability and cash flow because it greatly improves GMROI.

It increases turns. Slow moving merchandise is identified quickly, discounted earlier, and sold faster.

It increases gross margin. Merchandise is discounted by a lesser amount in steps according to how old it is. Simply put, the older the merchandise, the bigger the price discount. By doing it this way, you will sell more merchandise at a higher mark.

It increases sales and cash flow. Because your dogs will be sold faster, funds will be made available to try new merchandise items that may become best sellers. Once your salespeople see this system in action, they will love it. They will have greater product selection and be able to offer deals to their clients more often.

Finally, one of the most overlooked benefits of an efficient markdown system is that **it delivers free advertising.** Retailers who implement this properly, spend less money on advertising, because they harness the power of "word of mouth". When you give your customers "real" unexpected discounts (not during a clearance sale) they brag to their friends and show off your products! Their friends will remember and visit you when they are in the market. (This dog merchandise is not necessarily *unfashionable*, it just does not work in your retail environment).

Golden Steps with Implementing a Markdown System

1. Choose a project lead. This is one of the most important jobs in your company, as it significantly improves merchandise flow. This task should be given to a highly responsible person who has proven that he or she can successfully complete tasks on an ongoing basis. Your inventory manager/buyer should be able to lead in this capacity.

2. Define your levels. To do this, you need to set inventory aging dates. Setting six levels every 60 days is a great place to start. Many companies however, will be more heavily inventoried due to the absence of a working markdown system. If this is your case, you should set the periods further out so that no more than 25% of your inventory is marked down at any one time.

You will be able to tighten up the levels as you start seeing results and your inventory to sales ratio begins to fall. (This will occur provided you only buy new merchandise when you have a true open to buy). Faster turning retailers could markdowns every 30 days, for example. Some product segments have even faster schedules.

Consider defining a few different markdown schedules where products typically have different lifecycles. For example, you may find that one product category turns slower than other categories. This category may warrant a separate aging schedule. Or, it may be necessary to turn a certain product line faster with a quicker aging schedule.

A note on seasonal operations: Set the aging periods faster in certain times of the year and slower in other times. This helps augment the large fluctuations in customer traffic and inventory levels.

3. Define your "Golden Actions". Now that you have six markdown levels, you need to define what you will do at each level. Your actions should get progressively more aggressive, providing more incentive for customers to buy at each level. Be creative in your actions so that you can find what works best in your market. Here is an example of a markdown schedule:

Level 1: 60 days. Discount up to 10% (optional). This is the last chance for the item. Identify the merchandise. Check where it is displayed. Re-merchandise and move on the floor. Un-nail. Educate the sales manager and the salespeople.

Level 2: 120 days: Discount 20%. No more last chance. The merchandise must go. Salespeople can negotiate at will.

Level 3: 180 days: Discount 30%. Spiff.

Level 4: 240 days: Discount 40%. Move to clearance center or as-is area.

Level 5: 300 days: Discount 50%. Clearance center. Put on web page in your clearance section. Include a link in your monthly e-newsletter to the "HOT DEALS" section of your web site.

Level 6: 360 days: Discount 60%. Put up a "Below Cost" sign. Use for a weekend draw prizes. Use in BOGO (Buy One, Get One) type offers.

4. Perform your monthly duties. Each month, the above duties must be performed without exception, for all categories and vendors. To skip a month because you are too busy will cause the system to eventually fail. Expect implementation to take more time at the beginning. However, expect it to be less time-consuming and more manageable as time goes on and processes become routine.

5. Execute, refine, and never stop! Execution is the key to success. About 20% of the people who try to implement this system are successful and about 80% fail. That's Life. If you are confident and committed to improvement you can be in this top 20% and your profit will follow. Refine your "Golden Actions". Become a student of your business and find what works for you. If your periods are longer than 60 days, as your inventory drops, reduce the number of days to get the system moving faster. Make it fun and stay with it forever.

In conclusion, please remember that the system presented above is not a theory. It works. Just do it. Believe and execute!

16. OPEN TO BUY

To buy or not to buy?

When and what to buy are the critical starting points of whether an inventory carrying business will succeed. If you purchase too much too soon, then cash flow will be short. Extra inventory will result. It is a fact of life that the minority of the new untested merchandise that you buy will become best sellers. The majority will sit. At the same time though, you need to find winners by gambling on new purchases. The hot items make up the overwhelming majority of your sales and gross margin dollars.

Bottom line: without buying you have no sales, but with buying too much or not the right product at the right time you have less cash to buy.

This writing is about finding balance by understanding the components of an open to buy strategy.

My definition of open to buy is: when can you buy, approximately how much can you spend, and on what product you should focus your $$$ on.

In my opinion there is not a one size fits all open to buy equation. There are many factors which make one operation different from the next. The open to buy strategy should really be customized and then fine-tuned to meet an organization's needs. For example, a sporting goods retailer has different requirements than a home goods retailer. That said, here are some important common elements that should be considered as part of your open to buy strategy:

1. Special Orders: There is always open to buy – at the right margin. When a customer wants to order customized merchandise, for example, you should always order it, provided you mark up all your costs appropriately. Special order typically produce the highest gross margin return on inventory (GMROI) of any items when done right. You have super high turns due to the inventory coming in and then going out fast. You have high gross margin because custom orders can typically be priced higher than showroom merchandise. An extra markup makes good business sense as you provide additional value and incur extra processing costs on orders. You should require a minimum of 50% deposit (however always ask for the full amount).

2. Best Sellers: There is always open to buy for best sellers – before you are going to run out. This is when your stock of individual item quantities fall below your safety level. This is where you would run out of stock for your rate of sale and average lead time.

Make sure you determine your best sellers correctly. Best sellers can be defined as those items that produce the majority of your gross margin dollars. Ensure that you check stock levels, rate of sale and re-order lead times on these items and repurchase them before putting any money into new merchandise. Your odds will always be better betting on a winner before an untested item. Even if you are over inventoried in dogs and cash flow is short, you need to find the funds to reinvest here. Without investing in what works in your business you will face best seller stock outs and less sales volume as a result.

3. **Slow movers, and Dogs: There is NEVER open to buy here.** This seems obvious, right? Well, it's not because I've seen many buyers reorder items as soon they are sold off the floor. They use a min / max type of system that replenishes whenever they sell down to a certain quantity. They do not take into account how long the item has been sitting on the floor or the lead time. If one item takes 8 months to sell, for example, don't rebuy it. Put your money into proven best sellers, try new items instead or leave it in the bank.

4. **New Items: Are you under your target inventory to sales?** If no, you do not have open to buy, even if you have Warren Buffet type of cash. (By the way, people like Warren Buffet understand this.)

5. **Incoming new merchandise already on order:** Spreading out the timing of receipt is important with new merchandise. You should analyze the aging of incoming new merchandise orders. Project the next 30/60/90 days so that you don't have an unexpected over inventory and resulting short cash flow issue.

6. **Liquidity: Is your quick ratio decent?** Quick ratio is a measurement of cash flow that basically acts as a gauge as to whether you have enough cash to cover your short term obligations. (Quick Ratio = (Total Cash and Receivables) / Debt due under 1 year and customer deposits held) If you are lower than your target, .5-1 for example, you need to be extra careful with new purchases.

7. **Determine an open to buy dollar amount.** Provided that you have all your special order items and best-selling stock items on order and have a decent inventory to sales level you can figure a dollar amount that you could afford to spend on new merchandise. For instance if you are at 15% inventory to sales and you decide that the highest you can afford to be is 16% inventory to sales, determine what amount of extra stock will take you to that level. That is the maximum amount of extra inventory investment allowable. (Again, don't forget to take into

account lead times and the new merchandise already on order to ensure that you are not hit with a sudden glut of new items.)

8. **Product Type: Buy from strong areas.** When buying new merchandise review your GMROI on all categories and vendors within each category.

9. **Price Point: Look for opportunities in the gaps**. After you have determined your target categories and vendors to expand, review existing price points. If there are any gaps in bestselling price point areas, add there, first, when buying new merchandise.

10. **Now what**: Great inventory managers recognizes that the actions you take after the new merchandise arrives are just as important. To review I recommend:

    - Display fast on the showroom
    - Display fast on your web site
    - Merchandise in a high traffic area to get the best test
    - Educate your sales people
    - Price properly with respect to other items in your line up
    - Group / package price as well as individually price
    - Show other selling options on the price tags
    - Nail down (don't sell the last display item if you special order off them and they are best sellers)
    - If it works, reorder in appropriate quantity
    - If does not sell in 45-60 day, un-nail and drop from the lineup, then use the mark down system.

Try to take all these components into account when determining the best open to buy for your unique situation. Take emotion out of your equation and add analytics. Remember the name of the game is to sell the most, at the highest gross margin, with the smallest amount of inventory in stock

17. WHAT IS BAR CODING REALLY WORTH?

After visiting a client, I wanted to share with you how we answered an important inventory control question, "What is bar coding inventory worth?"

Let me give you some background. This business was a two store operation, had projected sales of $3.5 million, had 35,000 square feet in expanded showroom and operated a warehouse of 7,000 square feet. They were pursuing an aggressive sales growth strategy.

They had five decent performing warehouse employees (4 full time, 1 part time). They all pitched in on duties such as receiving, transfers, delivery routing/scheduling, picking, delivery, customer service, and physical inventory.

So, here was their dilemma: they wanted to become more efficient without hiring extra warehouse employees premature to their expected increase in sales.

Solution: Bar Code.

Fine, prove it. What is bar coding REALLY worth?

To do this, we looked at where time was spent doing manual tasks that bar coding would improve on.

Here was the conservative break down:

Receiving preparation – efficiency savings: 15 minutes per day; 65 hours per year (5 day week) minimum.

Manual Process: Printing receiving tallies and sold tags were necessary on the manual inventory control system because they listed what was ordered, gave a checklist, and identified what was being received for customers.

Bar code: Now all they would need to do would be to print and sort the bar code labels ahead of the merchandise arriving. The customers' names were on the bar code labels. Sold tags were not necessary. The exact item would be known due to a unique bar code tracking ID.

Physical receiving – efficiency savings: 30 minutes per day; 130 hours per year minimum.

Manual: As the merchandise came off the truck, they checked off the bill of lading, filled out the receiving tallies, and applied the non-bar code tags to the merchandise.

Bar code: With bar coding, they would scan and apply the bar code labels as the merchandise entered the warehouse. This would be their check and balance. If there were any labels remaining, they were short shipped. If they did not have enough labels, they were over shipped. Any discrepancies would be noted and the bill of lading signed.

Computer receiving – efficiency savings: 45 minutes per day; 195 hours per year minimum.

Manual: From the receiving lists, a data entry person entered all information into the software one purchase order at a time. They would then edit and confirm (post) into the IT system.

Bar code: Significant time would be saved since all their items would be uploaded from the scanner either via batch or wireless connectivity. They would only check their piece count for missed scans. The use of inventory holding areas would also act as an automatic double check of accuracy as they could be easily reconciled at any time.

Transfers – efficiency savings: 1 hour per day; 260 hours per year minimum.

Manual: To enable merchandise to be found after they received it, they needed to manually assign it to locations. This involved their warehouse employees writing down each item and the location every time they moved it. Then a data entry person transferred each location move in the computer. Timeliness is crucial and they were always behind.

Bar code: They would simply scan each item as it is moved and upload to their system. Wireless technology would make this real-time.

Merchandising Picking, preparation, and Customer pick-ups – efficiency savings: 1+ hour minimum per day; 260+ hours per year minimum.

Manual: It was common that warehouse employees were forced to look around for merchandise prior to delivery or when a customer came to pick up their product. This was embarrassing and very costly. Item locations need to be exact.

Bar code: This would enable them to find their merchandise FAST. It would vastly improve customer service. The value of this alone was worth implementing bar code systems and procedures.

Physical inventory – efficiency savings: 160+ hours per year minimum.

Manual: To do a proper complete manual stock check, it

involved many people and several teams. They would write down each item in their area. Mistakes were inevitable. Then, a data entry team would reconcile and fix quantities and locations in their system. They might even shut their stores down.

This kind of inventory was NEVER accurate and it took a huge amount of time. This hated practice was only done once per year – which caused additional inaccuracy since counts got worse as the year progressed.

Bar code: They would never need to take a full physical inventory again. WOOHOO!!! They would schedule and perform proper cycle aisle and location inventories. There would not be any more hand writing. The comparative reconciliation process between perpetual (before scanning) and actual (after scanning) would be automatic!

Selling – savings: unquantifiable, it's MASSIVE.

Is there a more important time to know exactly where merchandise is than when a customer wants to buy it? How many times do salespeople call the warehouse to physically check for the availability of merchandise? Are there sold tags in the warehouse? Ask these questions of your operation.

Theft and Shrinkage – savings: 5% of inventory value minimum.

Simply put, it is much easier to steal merchandise if the quantities and locations are wrong. Criminals know this. Bar coding effectively closes the theft door. The adoption of proper bar code procedures is the best way to control your largest asset. Do you know how much shrinkage you have?

The WOW CUSTOMERS bonus – become a retail leader, not a follower!

Features with wireless bar coding enable sales associates to perform merchandise lookups and add items to sales using shopping cart features. Do you want to stay ahead of your competition in the WOW factor?

So, what is bar coding REALLY worth?

For this retailer of $3.5 Million in sales, the gain in efficiency alone was at least 1,070+ hours of labor and 5% of inventory value per year minimum. The other gains in sales advantages, and wowing customers would be even more!

18. GET VENDOR CREDITS

Whether you sell furniture, bicycles, or cars, customers expect and deserve their merchandise to be free of all damages and defects.

Let's put ourselves in the customer's shoes for a minute:

You paid a deposit for a new living room set complete with gorgeous leather seating and mahogany tables. Two months later you finally get the set delivered to your home, after waiting patiently for two hours on a workday. The delivery crew is professional and courteous, placing your new furniture exactly where you want it. Everything looks great so you sign the paperwork and give them a check for the remaining amount. Later that evening you sit down to relax on your new sofa. Then, you spot a scratch in the wood on your coffee table. How do you feel?

To meet these quality standards, you as a retailer, should ensure products are defect free, prior to giving them to the customer. Any cost that you incur to rectify a defect should be passed on to your vendors where appropriate.

Here are some actions you can take to maximize your legitimate vendor charge backs (VCBs) and keep your customers happy:

• Establish and train a customer service coordinator who is on an incentive program.

• Setup the systems and procedures for tracking and reporting service issues within your software program.

• Require product inspection on receiving. "Deluxe" product prior to shipping, delivery or pick-up.

• Have your service tech write up all product repairs that are legitimate vendor damages, on a shop repair form, and take a picture, prior to the repair. Do this every day!

• Require your service coordinator to enter these repairs as credit requests into your service system.

• Email the VCB (Vendor Charge Back) invoice and picture to your vendor contact.

• Establish an open vendor credit request file for easy review.

• During meetings with product reps, have your buyer discuss the open service file, first, before talking about purchasing.

• Ask your reps to sign credit authorizations for all concessions given.

• Ensure that your buyers, service coordinator, and payable clerks communicate closely and notify each other when credits are authorized. Organized email and project sharing systems like MS SharePoint, Dropbox, and Evernote are great for communication.

• Run an open vendor credit request report monthly to see which requests are unresolved. Resend them. If they become older than two or three months with no answer, take your credit.

• Enter all vendor charge backs or credits in Accounts Payable. Provide a reference with your next check.

• Review your financials monthly for VCB revenue. You should see service income steadily increase!

I should mention that these steps are not intended to punish your vendors or hurt any relationships. They are purely intended to align your expectations with those of your customers and make your vendors responsible to that level. In the process, if done properly, you could see 1% to 2 % of your costs recaptured in vendor credits. You will also be in a better position to meet your customers' quality requirements.

19. MARGINS ARE IN YOUR HEAD

The Art and Science of Increasing Gross Margin

The most common objection I get from business managers when I suggest that their margins can be improved is, "We can't increase our prices. We have too much competition and we will lose sales!"

Sorry, that excuse does not fly. It has been proven to be wrong over and over again. In the performance groups that I lead, many retail businesses approach 50 percent gross margin and some are over 60 percent! All these businesses are in competitive markets. In this writing, I am going to discuss some of the practices that successful retailers use to maximize margins.

The first thing to understand is that margins are in your head. You achieve the margins that you do because that is what you think you can get. It's like the saying, **"If you think you can or if you think you can't, you are right"**. If you believe that you should price all merchandise at "a number" (50 margin or 100 markup), then that is the most you will get. Ever! In fact, you will probably get between 42 and 45 percent at the most, due to discounting. To break the 50 percent barrier the old "number" pricing practice needs to be thrown in the garbage. Open your mind to pricing and you will make a ton extra.

You see, outside of products that are fixed cost commodities with no substitutions, margins are flexible. To the consumer, the product is worth what they pay for it. To the salesperson, it is worth what they sell it for. If a customer buys an item for $499 from a salesperson, neither of them really care whether you bought that item for $200 or $250. If product value and great customer service are in place, and there is no easy comparison point, the price can be flexible.

I can hear you questioning me now, "But, there is a comparison point. Our competitor carries the same thing. People shop around. And, what about the internet?"

Right, customers do shop around and if you make it more attractive to do business with you, they will shop with you more than your competition. And, you really don't have to make it that easy to shop you... do you?

Margins are both Art and Science

They are an art form in that you can be flexible in your pricing techniques. You can use different approaches for different items. One size does not fit all in art. **Be creative.**

Margins are a science too because at the end of the day the mathematical equation of (price sold - landed cost purchased) / price sold is what you get. Your results should be studied from a non-emotional level. **Be analytical.**

Following are some art and some science practices that have been used successfully to increase gross margins.

Don't let your software system be your only guide.

For pricing on newly received merchandise, don't let your computer be the final determination of your selling price. The human element in pricing is critical. For example, if you want to achieve approximately a 50 percent margin for a particular vendor, set a cost multiplier of 2.25 over landed. That would deliver a 55.5 margin for that price. So, if an item cost $200, the system would spit out a price of $450. Then the buyer should physically look at the item and ask, "Does this price make sense? Or, should it be priced more or maybe less?" In this case, if the buyer believes the item could fetch $499 it should be changed in the system. Then the price tag should be printed. If you let a computer be the sole determinant of the final price, you will end up with odd ball pricing and leave a lot of dollars on the table. It is well worth the extra work. A few extra dollars here and there will add up to thousands of dollars in additional profits.

Price point.

One of the first things I do when visiting a store is to walk the showroom. I look at the price points. When I do this, I don't even need to see costs to come up with extra margin. Often, I will notice bizarre price points. For example, product will be offered at $209 instead of $199, or $1230 instead of $1,299. This most often occurs because a strict computerized formula is being followed. Businesses that produce the highest margins are flexible in their pricing.

There is an exception here: Where odd-ball pricing is the intention and margin potential is being maximized. Retailers who follow this strategy claim there is a psychological effect of odd-ball pricing on customers.

Price best sellers right.

Analytics are important. It is most often the case that the minority of the products that you offer contribute to the majority of gross margin dollars (aka 80/20 principle). Knowing and pricing these best sellers properly is critical. Routinely, pull best seller item detail reports from your ERP (enterprise resource planning) system. Look at the retail price and the gross margin percentage produced. Check to see if the prices make sense for best sellers. These items are proven to sell and a few percentage points in gross margin rarely make a difference to customers. It does however make a big difference to your business over time.

Stock best sellers more often.

If you agree with me that winning items produce the lion's share of gross margin dollars, you will also agree with me that if you keep them available in front of customers and salespeople, you will sell more of these items. Here, it is a numbers game. Higher best seller in stock days equals greater gross margin dollars.

Value price on custom jobs and special orders.

Buying something as is, off the shelf is easy for transaction processing. If the customer wants it the way they see it, they pay for it and they take it home. There are few additional inventory expenses for the company as the costs are sunk (incurred already). Anytime there is a customized change in how the customer wants the product, extra costs are incurred by the business. There are increased time costs with the salesperson organizing the order, purchasing costs, freight costs, warehousing costs, distribution expenses, and sometimes additional service costs.

Often times I see that businesses charge the same price as if they were selling an in-stock item. I suggest charging a higher mark up for customization and / or a distribution fee. This is an additional service you are rendering. If you want a really simple way to do this, just tell your salespeople the new policy is to charge 2.5 x vendor catalogue cost, for example. It is okay to charge more if you are giving additional value.

Private label.

Do you have a good name brand in your market area? If so, you should have a private label program. There is no direct comparison for consumers, and there are countless vendors around the world and maybe even locally that can help you achieve a lower cost and higher margin. Whether you are selling furniture, mattresses, accessories, clothing, or pet food, you should have a private label line. Whether you cater to high society or the blue collar customer, you should have a private label line.

If you don't feel like your name brand is the way to go, make up a brand. When sourcing suppliers I suggest that you look for these key elements: past private label success, extended terms, quick shipping lead times, product support, brand comparable quality or better. Your private label brand does not need to be the cheapest product. It can be at any price point level that you offer. Some very successful businesses have exclusive high end lines and achieve large margin percentages and dollars in that space.

Private label branded merchandise.

Most of you reading this carry national brands. All of you hate getting shopped. Whether it is an internet business or your competitor across the street, consumers find it easier than ever these days, to shop you. They can just pull up their smart phone and use one of the many apps to search your product. There is a fairly simple way to deter this. Just stop putting your real model numbers or style names on the products that you are being shopped on. For example, if an item is called the "Hemingway Chair", you might rename it the "Fisherman's Lounger" on the price tag. Your software system will most likely have an extra field you can use to accomplish this.

A word of caution. Don't rename everything. You need the real branded models too on various products. And, consider pricing select products at a low margin so you can encourage price shopping that will result in your prices being much better than the competition. One client actually encourages price shopping on their web site. They say on their home page: "Come in and our salespeople will help you price shop on their iPads." Now that's confidence. By the way, their margins are above all their direct competitors.

Buy with a mission rather than your gut.

Often buyers attend trade shows without a clear strategy. Sometimes people show up with just a vague idea of how much money they would like to spend, and then roll the dice on what they feel is the next hot thing. They are primarily concerned about the cost of the item and later figure what they can sell it for. They price, using cost plus. If this is how you approach buying, try this at your next show:

Put aside a certain dollar amount for your open to buy. Before leaving for the show, produce a best seller report. Find out which price points are producing. Figure out where the gaps are (the empty slots). Plan on which price points (or slots) to add to your lineup. Then, when you go to the trade show, look for merchandise that you think you can sell at whatever price points you have open. Lastly, look at the cost. What's your margin? If it is more than expected and the terms are good, give it a shot.

Mark down slow moving merchandise on a quick schedule.

We all know that discounting and blow out events hurt margins. Businesses that sell at a more consistent rate, without having to go deep into their profitability pockets several times per year, end up with much higher cash flow. The key is proper inventory management and focus on GMROI (gross margin return on inventory). With respect to margins, one field-proven way to increase gross margin is to mark down in incremental steps sooner. This enables faster selling of non-gross margin producing inventory. You should set up an aging on your inventory that pulls out the $0 gross margin producers. Then, you should initiate an associated mark-down percent that is related to the days aged. For example, if an item does not produce in 45 days of carrying, then an automatic markdown of 10 percent may be executed. If it does not sell in another 45 days, an additional 10 percent discount may be applied.

If that item was then sold at the 20 percent discount in 90 days, it is still a lot more productive than if the item was stocked for 365 days and finally sold at 50 percent off. You would have gained extra margin, faster turns, and a new opportunity to free up floor or shelf space to try a new item that might produce. Bottom line - it is better to turn and burn than to hold and lose.

Incentivize high gross margin sales.

If you believe people will do what you lead and pay them to do, this will work for you. If people are not led or paid right, it may not work. Here is the practice: instead of paying a straight commission percent on the sale, pay a variable percent.

The key is that the variable percent is determined by the gross margin percentage sold. This can have a huge impact on profitability. It can almost eliminate using negotiation and discounting as a salesperson's tool. When implementing, it is important to set a spread between a high commission rate and a low commission rate of at least 5 points. The high is tied to high gross margin sales, say 60 percent and above. The low commission rate is tied to low gross margin sales, say 30 percent. Everything in between is on a variable rate.

Note that this is only an example and any business setting this up must analyze its individual model first to determine the proper rates to maximize gross margin. Most businesses that have implemented this system say that they have increased margins between three and nine percent. Combine this type of incentive program with a team bonus and a pay for performance and your team will succeed in delivering higher margins.

There are more ways to increase margins.

Try to be both analytical and creative and you can find them for your unique situation. It is worth the work, as the improvement has a direct impact on your net income and cash flow at the end of the day.

What was that objection again? Oh, something about "can't" and not increasing prices for fear of lost sales and competition? Don't fear. You deserve to make a healthy margin for the value that you give. Margins are in your head.

20. DIGITAL INVENTORY SMART STEPS

About a year ago, my wife decided that she wanted to redo our kitchen. The first stage was dreaming and visualization. To get help, she googled "kitchen planning". She chose to use Ikea's Home Planner, as it seemed the best for her needs. As her design progressed, she started to source specific items from various retailers. These included appliances, cabinets, flooring, lighting, wall tile, furniture, countertops, and trades people. She googled many hours into the night.

Her product search worked basically like this, she started general and then got specific. At first she browsed broad categories of merchandise (online and then in-store). Then she narrowed it down to specific vendors and exact models or styles. Once she found her favorite items, she googled vendor model numbers. Local lists of retailers that carried these items appeared on Google. She visited these sites and signed up to receive their e-newsletters. She then checked each piece to determine the best price and availability of merchandise. When she needed more information, she either used live chat, sent an email or called the retailer's customer service number.

After her initial research was done she was ready to buy. She bought from several different retailers. In some cases, she visited their physical stores to make some purchases. In other cases, she bought online for convenience. The majority of her purchases came from local retailers where both their merchandise availability and prices were listed on their web site. However, two appliance purchases were made from a retailer based in New York. All items shipped directly to our home in San Diego for a total of $59 in delivery charges.

This example is typical of the shopping behaviors of 30-something home goods consumers. It illustrates why your internet inventory strategy should be a critical part of your overall advertising program. It is an essential element that will drive your future traffic and sales success.

Considerations in Internet Inventory Strategy:

- Google is the top advertising network.
- Getting your product listed on Google is vital. It increases the chance that consumers will visit you when they are ready to buy, increasing your traffic.
- Consumers know how to use product preview planners. You need one and you need to learn how to use it. I.e. furniture stores have room planners, car dealers have auto planners, and clothing stores have size charts and interactive color swatches.
- Consumers often shop online before they visit a physical store.
- Consumers search for specific vendors, models, features, and styles. An up-to-date catalog of the merchandise you carry needs to be on your site. Your customers may get lost on your site (and disappointed) if you display merchandise that you no longer carry.
- Your customers will be comparing you to your competitors who carry the same models.
- Consumers will buy online and offline. However, in many cases, they will find you first online.
- There is little loyalty to brands or retailers. Top customer service, availability of product on your site, fast delivery, and great prices are all expected. If you do not deliver that, consumers will use Google to find someone that does.
- People read and write reviews. You should monitor and be and active participant in popular sites like Yelp.

How can you take advantage of these lessons, beat your competition, and capitalize on higher traffic that leads to greater sales?

In the operations section of this book, I described 5 Retail SMART steps. Now, to help you develop a strategy to attract today's tech-minded consumers, here are 5 SMART steps with a digital inventory:

1. Show in-stock inventory on your website.
2. Make communicating and buying convenient.
3. Automate and integrate.
4. Reinvent and innovate.
5. Touch your audience.

SMART Step 1
Show your in-stock inventory on your website.

Content attracts hits. If the consumer does not find you on the first page of Google, you may not exist to them. Take this test: while in your physical store, google your top product category. Then google a few top selling items. Does your store come up on the first page? If it does, congratulations. You are probably working hard to catalog inventory content on your website. If your store is not coming up when googling, you may be losing traffic because consumers are visiting your competitors, rather than you, when they search.

Google matches search terms with relevant website content and takes into account the proximity of the store and consumer. Those with web sites that display the inventory information that consumers are searching for, have a better chance of getting in-store traffic. What information do consumers want? Price, in-stock status, color options, warranty information, size, shipping, related items, purchasing, delivery options, and more. Consumers want it all.

SMART Step 2
Make Communicating and Buying Convenient.

Today's consumers want real-time information on your merchandise. They don't like to wait. However, they will often need your assistance while shopping online. Here are some essential online inventory components:

Telephone inquiries. There should be a telephone number on your website that connects consumers to someone in customer service. In this case "customer service" refers to someone in sales. Offline retail has a bad habit of equating customer service with problem resolution. Customer service, to a customer, means help with anything. Your website should have a unique 800 telephone number for your site that routes consumers directly to your sales professionals. This way they can assist the online shopper properly. You can also easily track, manage, and review calls that come from this number on your website.

Email or text inquiries. Your customer should be able to easily find your sales/service email address and text number. A salesperson should respond in less than 18 hours to any email inquiry. Text responses should be fairly immediate during business hours.

Live chat. Live chat allows your customers to speak with you via keyboard while they are looking at your site. In an age of multi-taskers, consumers often prefer this over email or the telephone. It's similar to online texting.

E-newsletter sign-up. This allows consumers to get information sent to them about your latest specials and ideas. People will often sign up in the dreaming stages of the purchase cycle.

Related products. Consumers want to see complementary or matching product. This is a key component when helping them shop. It will increase your average sale size.

Wish lists. When people are going through the final selection process, they routinely add and change products. Allow customers to do this themselves on your site. Wish lists are quotes. Quotes lead to sales.

Buy now. The purchasing decision will often come at a time when the consumer is not in your store. A husband and wife may just say one evening, over a glass of wine, "Let's just buy this before someone else does and save ourselves the hassle of going down to the store." Your web site should be ecommerce enabled.

SMART Step 3
Automate and integrate.

An objective should be to maintain a like image of your physical showroom on the internet. There are two ways to move your product information and pictures from your offline database to your online store.

You can hire people to update your site daily. They would need to review and compare your offline and online inventory constantly and change information as needed.

The second option is to automate and integrate your inventory. Basically the way to accomplish this is to create a communication system that allows your software to talk with your online shopping cart. The data and pictures are extracted and uploaded from your data server to your web server. Newly stocked items are added. Changes are made. Out of stock items are removed – automatically. There are innovative software partners out there that help you accomplish this.

Customers get up-to-date information and web content is made available for Google to advertise your business.

SMART Step 4
Reinvent & innovate.

I'm sure that many of you would agree that the return on traditional advertising such as TV, radio and newspaper, has been declining. Countless retailers still spend money on the same old advertising media while their traffic and sales have declined. I've also seen some businesses innovate themselves and get a higher ROI on their advertising. This is due to the fact that consumers' focus has shifted - to internet media. Retail and e-tail are merging together as one.

Retailers that have grown the most over that past 10 years are those that have innovated on the web. A prime example of an inventory carrying retailer that has succeeded is Zappos. It has grown to over a billion dollars in sales.

There were two critical transitions that helped lead to Zappos' success.

One was that they reinvented their business model and web site to display in-stock inventory. Initially, this decreased the amount of products and vendors shown. However, it assisted their customers by focusing them on what was available for immediate sale. Zappos sales tripled after they started carrying and showing the right inventory on their web site.

The second transition was that Zappos changed their core business values, establishing an out of this world customer service model. The words "WOW" and "delivering happiness" are infused throughout their entire organization.

Great retailers like Zappos continually seek self-improvement. This is why they grow and prosper. If you haven't innovated your business model in a while, now is the time to do so.

SMART Step 5
Touch your audience.

The more often you "touch" your customers with value, the greater your opportunity to make sales will be. This makes for happy customers. Communicating with value means: helping customers to navigate the various steps of their shopping experience. You make their buying decision easier by helping, rather than selling. If you do this, your customers will become your friends. Your friends will advertise for you for FREE. They use the best media ever: word-of-mouth advertising.

There are some really fantastic ways that you can use your web inventory system to help you accomplish this. To demonstrate how you can touch your audience with value, follow this scenario:

- Mrs. Smith is sitting in her home office. She thinks that she would like a more stylish look. Like that one she saw on her favorite TV show. She starts to look around – at friend's houses, at various stores, and through general web browsing.
- Mrs. Smith googles brands, models, styles of desks that she likes.
- She finds one exact desk displayed on your web site listed on the first page of Google. (value touch 1)
- She clicks the link. She is taken directly to that desk's individual landing page in your online store. (value touch 2)
- Mrs. Smith sees the related items (bookshelf, chair, and lamp) that go with the desk. (value touch 3)
- She then has a question about the type of wood that the desk is made of. She clicks on your live chat button. She is connected instantly to a customer service representative at your store. In another minute she has her question answered – solid wood mahogany. (value touch 4)
- She is not ready to buy yet. She wants to get a list of pricing for all the pieces (the desk, bookshelf, lamp, and chair) so that she can discuss it with her husband. She adds all the items to her wish list on your site. Then she prints out her "quote". (value touch 5)
- Mrs. Smith discusses her office with her husband. They are not sure how the items will look or fit. So, they go back to your online store. They use your product planner to get a better idea. They then print the diagram out. (value touch 6)
- Mrs. Smith signs up to your VIP email list on your site in case you have any upcoming sales. She would also like to check out your e-newsletter. (value touch 7)
- Mr. and Mrs. Smith have some final questions on the delivery vs. pick up service. They easily find your telephone

number and email listed on every page of your site. They call your customer service number and talk to a designer, Lynne. Lynne helps them with the final information that they need. Lynne offers to email the info. She gets Mrs. Smith's contact info while on the telephone. (value touch 8)

- Lynne sends a thank you email to Mrs. Smith, recaps the telephone call, and gives the hours that she is working. She invites them to drop by or call again. (value touch 9)
- Mr. and Mrs. Smith go on vacation and forget all about their home office and your store for a couple of weeks.
- You send out a monthly follow-up email to Lynne's customers with open quotes/wish lists. Mrs. Smith gets this reminder. It contains a 5% off offer valid for one month. Mrs. Smith saves that email. (value touch 10)
- The Smiths get all their research together and visit your physical store.They ask for Lynne,by name. (value touch 11)
- Lynne and the Smiths review the online quote and plan. They look at the actual product. The sale is completed. (value touch 12)
- After the merchandise is delivered you email your daily customer satisfaction surveys. Mr. and Mrs. Smith receive theirs. The Smiths are happy. (value touch 13)
- They tell their friends, "the Jones". (value touch 14)

Today, consumers initiate their shopping experience. Often this starts with Google. If they find you, you have a chance of getting their business. If they do not find you on Google, you may be invisible. If you give information and "WOW" people, your word-of-mouth advertising could sky rocket.

Use SMART Steps of Digital Inventory Management to help you achieve higher traffic and a better return on your inventory and advertising investment.

1. Show in-stock inventory on your website.
2. Make communicating and buying convenient.
3. Automate and integrate.
4. Reinvent and innovate.
5. Touch your audience.

21. IGMROI & CRM

Tips for expanding or contracting product lines

IGMROI stands for Incremental Gross Margin Return on Inventory. It takes the GMROI metric a step further. Tracking IGMROI can help you assess product expansions or contractions. It also can help you better understand consumer buying patterns. Its purpose is to assist you in establishing a more customer-relevant product mix that increases your sales.

CRM stands for Customer Relationship Management. It consists of systems that allow for the recording of customer behavior and sales data. It allows a business to manage their relationships better.

Consumer's tastes and the economy are constantly changing. Some vendors and categories that were once popular are not anymore. You cannot control your customer's tastes or the economy. People decide on their own. I believe that people like to buy what they want and hate being sold something else. If you agree, ask yourself, "What can I control then?"

If you can manage a process, you can influence and control it. So, by better understanding your customers buying patterns and establishing a more related product mix, you will satisfy more people and sell more.

Crunching the Numbers

First, take some of the guessing out of the equation. There is only one group's opinion, regarding the desirability of purchasing your products, that matters. It's not your buyers, your reps, suppliers or your competition. And, it's not you or me. It's your customers!

Buying is analytical. You should know what your customers are purchasing, now. You should seek to know what they may want to buy from you in the future. With CRM software, this data could become available to you. CRM systems allow for imputing and tracking of next purchase desires, project management, related items, and customer follow up. Also, changes in past purchase trends can be indicative of the future. You can use this business information to hedge your product expansion and contraction bets.

To find out what current tastes are, analyze your sales data over the last several months and rank your vendors underneath each category. By doing this, you will see what categories and vendors are your customers' favorites.

Now, don't forget to look at the Gross Margin Return on Inventory of each of these categories and vendors. As a reminder, GMROI is the amount of annualized gross margin dollars you make per dollar of inventory that you have invested ($GM/$IN).

With this data in hand you will see what your customers are buying and how profitable you really are. Your GMROI will tell you which area of your inventory has the greatest return.

Expanding and Contracting Product Lines

Now suppose your data points you in the direction of expanding a certain product line, vendor or category. You may wish to test the result of the expansion before committing to it over the long-term. That is where the measure of IGMROI comes in.

After two months of testing a product expansion (or contraction), look at your new GMROI in that vendor or category. Take the difference before and after, and then figure the GMROI on the increment or change.

IGMROI Formula

(New Gross Margin $ annualized – Old Gross Margin $ annualized) / (New Inventory $ - Old Inventory $) = IGRMOI.

Suppose a business decides to expand a certain supplier's category by $25,000 from an old inventory level of $50,000. Now suppose the expansion produced an extra $75,000 in gross margin dollars from a previous annualized gross margin of $200,000. Was the expansion a good idea? Let's see:

($275,000 – $200,000) / ($75,000 – $50,000) = $3.00 IGMROI

$3 is the amount of extra GMROI produced by the expansion. It alone does not tell you if the expansion was good or not. It must be compared with the GMROI's before and after.

IGMROI Rule:

If your incremental GMROI dips below your average GMROI, or below an attainable GMROI in another category, then you should not expand to the extent of the test.

Old GMROI = Old GM $ annualized / Old $ Inventory = $200,000 / $50,000 = $4.00

New GMROI = New GM $ annualized / New $ Inventory = $275,000 / $75,000 = $3.67

So, GMROI as a result of the expansion fell from $4.00 to $3.67. The Incremental GMROI of $3 fell below the new average GMROI of $3.67.

It is therefore dragging down the GMROI on average. The expansion should be discontinued unless the $3 IGMROI is still better than overall company averages or better than in other categories.

The name of the game is making the most money from the least amount of inventory investment while satisfying your customer's wants. Don't dwell on external forces. Use your CRM data to help you make better decisions and use metrics to help you measure your decisions. Focus internally on your situation. Manage what you can control.

22. ADD $250,000 GROSS MARGIN DOLLARS – *WITHOUT RAISING PRICES*

Did the headline catch your attention? If so, you will want to know that this feat can be accomplished by thinking outside the box through focusing on distribution efficiencies. Increasing the speed and effectiveness of handling merchandise can cause your cash flow and profit to take off. This is due to a higher return on your investment and a reduction in associated inventory carrying costs.

From the traditional GMROI formula of gross margin / inventory, it is simple to see that if you just increase gross margin and decrease inventory you will increase your return on investment. The trouble with using this easy to understand equation is that the actions to make gross margin go up or inventory go down are sometimes less than creative.

To increase GM, many people automatically think of increasing price or not selling at discounts. And, to decrease inventory on hand, clearance sales or sweeping discounts are a favorite. Unfortunately, these are counterproductive strategies, as gross margins are often offset. Clearance sales may have their time and place, however, there are many other more productive ways to increase GMROI, and you can do it without increasing prices or holding inventory clearance sales.

133

An alternative GMROI formula

Using "the other" formula for gross margin return on inventory, additional ways to produce a return become clearer.

> **GMROI = Turns x (Gross margin % / Cost of goods %)**

The secret is that by flowing your inventory faster (higher turns), you can obtain a much higher GMROI. So what's it worth?

Let's look at the two examples in Figures 1 and 2, and keep gross margin constant at 45%.

Figure 1

> **Store A**
>
> **Turns = 3 times per year**
>
> **Number of days to turn inventory = 365 / 3 = 121 days**
>
> **Store B**
>
> **Turns = 3.3 times per year**
>
> **Number of days to turn inventory = 365 / 3.3 = 110 days**

Figure 2

> **Store A**
>
> **GMROI = 3 turns x (45% GM / 55% COGS) = \$2.45**
>
> **Store B**
>
> **GMROI = 3.3 turns x (45% GM / 55% COGS) = \$2.70**

What's the Difference? In Figure 1, store B turns inventory 11 days faster than Store A. So, .3 extra turns a year equates to 11 days. Doesn't seem like much, right?

Now, let's look at the GMROI impact of flowing inventory 11 days faster in Figure 2.

What's the Difference? In Figure 2, store B makes .25 cents more for every dollar it invests in inventory than store A. So, what's that value of a quarter? It's MASSIVE!!!

<u>At $1 million in inventory, 25 cents in GMROI is equal to $250,000 in gross margin produced!</u>

Using the traditional GMROI formula of GM $ / Inventory $, and holding inventory constant, some simple algebra shows us that the increase in GM $ is: GMROI Increase x Inventory Value GM $ Increase = 25 cents x $1 million = $ 250,000 in additional gross margin dollars.

Where else can you find $250,000 lying around?

Do you think it is worth it to try to improve your merchandise flow efficiency so you can turn your inventory 11 days faster? Of course it is!

Ways to get your 11 days and an extra $250,000:

Quick Ship: Margins are not everything. Speed matters. Vendors that allow for faster order fulfillment permit retailers to carry less inventory. The best example of this I've seen is an Australian retailer with a small manufacturing plant that can deliver custom, high end contemporary seating to customers within 1 week.

Fast Receiving: Don't let merchandise sit on your dock un-received in your IT system. Use the latest technology to get counts recorded into your inventory. The fastest operations are receiving via wireless scanners as merchandise is unloaded. This creates a culture of zero delay within a business. Real-time processing is normally best.

Speedy Delivery Scheduling: Implement systems that show what merchandise can be scheduled, so you can book delivery times with customers as fast as possible. You should work towards having a high majority of your completed sales scheduled. Some retailers even schedule outgoing shipments prior to receiving---you really need to be confident in your vendors timeliness and quality to accomplish this.

Routing and Mapping Automation for Delivery: Use automated mobile systems to schedule faster, fill trucks easier, and take the best routing. The benefits are faster customer delivery and significantly reduced costs.

Improve Customer Pick-up's: As with deliveries, contact customers immediately to set times for merchandise pick-up. Companies that do this are seen as being more professional, saving their customers and themselves time.

Display all Merchandise – FAST: This is an area where many operations can use improvement. How can you sell something if you do not display it? Build a process similar to this:

- Create a listing of all available merchandise that is in your warehouse but not on display (every day).
- Create transfer orders.
- Physically check merchandise and determine the best price points.
- Put new merchandise in high traffic floor slots to properly test value in front of customers.

Efficient Customer Service: The return and repair process should be systematized so that it is quick for both employees and customers. You should know exactly how many customer service issues are outstanding, what needs to be repaired, and what needs to be replaced.

You do not want damaged or opened (unpackaged) merchandise choking your profits. One of my clients runs daily reports for opened items and takes actions to minimize dead inventory. Thus they maximize turns. This company estimates that this practice alone saves him over $50,000 per year.

Best Seller Recognition: Great managers track winning merchandise and respective rates of sale, so that they can reorder at the right time and in the appropriate quantity. Having proven product available for your customers using JIT (just-in-time) systems, rather than JIC (just-in-case) systems, dramatically increases turns. How? By increasing sales, decreasing lead times and minimizing unnecessary stock.

Burn Non-Sellers: "If it doesn't sell in 30 days, take it out to the front lawn and BURN IT!" This advice is from an exemplary retailer who gets a huge GMROI and great sales per square foot.

Buy New Merchandise - At the Right Time: Create an "open to buy" that acts as your traffic light when bringing on new items. Red is when you are over inventoried, yellow is on the edge, and green is when you are at an efficient GMROI, or Inventory to Sales. Best practice businesses use these metrics to determine the timing of their new purchasing.

Get Your People up to Speed as Industry Professionals: Just like you get a lawyer to handle your legal issues and a licensed tax professional to handle your taxes, get an industry expert to help develop your team. Productive, educated, and motivated people that produce results, are necessary for success.

So there you have it: 11 ways that can help you turn your inventory 11 days faster and maximize GMROI. Implement these ideas and you can make an extra $250,000 in GM per million in inventory invested.

Financial

23. THINK PROFIT!

Part 1 P&L Analysis

There is only one way to be successful in business. It's to Profit.

There is only one way to build cash in the bank. It's to Profit.

And, there is only one way to grow your business. It's to Profit.

Profitability sometimes takes a back seat to sales. It should not. Sales volume is a critical and necessary part of the profit equation, but it is just a part. Cash is only accumulated through the consistent spread that is made after the sale of an asset. That spread, or bottom line, needs to be in the 7%+ area every year to nicely accumulate cash.

Profit fuels growth. It is the driver of even higher sales and higher profit volume levels. This is because growth comes from investing in great people, inventory, facilities, systems, training, and marketing. The least expensive and least risky capital for this growth investment typically comes from equity in the business. And equity comes from either profit or an investor's pocket. The alternate source of funds for growth is debt. You probably agree that it is far more enjoyable to use profit to perpetuate business growth, rather than paying off loans. (even though interest on debt is a tax deductible expense)

In the real world of retail, I've seen thousands of financial statements: the great, the so-so, and the abysmal. One commonality is that businesses always have room for improvement. And also, the smallest improvements can have massive impacts on profitability.

This writing will cover the basics of how to analyze one of the three critical financial statements: the Profit and Loss (the other two presented later are the Balance Sheet and the Statement of Cash Flow).

Case Study

Following is a sample store P&L. This version of the Profit and Loss statement is called a common-sized statement. It enables the analysis with past periods, with peer companies for performance groups, and with an industry as a whole.

Company Background

- Independently owned and operated retailer.
- One store operation with one detached warehouse.
- Shareholders own the buildings separately and the business pays rent to them.
- 25,000 square foot showroom.
- Eight salespeople, one sales manager.
- Average sale = $1,350; traffic count for the year = 18,519; close rate = 20%.
- $1,000,000 average inventory at cost.
- Vendor merchandising – mid to upper end price points.
- Special order percentage of sale volume = 50%.
- Budgeted sales for the year: $5.26 Million.

Profit and Loss for the Year End

		Dec. 31, (20XX)	% of Sales
Sales 1234	$	5,000,000	100.00%
Cost of Goods Sold	$	2,800,000	56.00%
Gross Margin	$	2,200,000 ⑤	44.00%
Operating Expenses			
Administrative	$	510,000	10.20%
Occupancy	$	400,000 ⑥	8.00%
Advertising & Marketing	$	350,000	7.00%
Selling	$	435,000 ⑦	8.70%
Service	$	50,000 ⑧	1.00%
Warehouse	$	155,000	3.10%
Delivery	$	88,000 ⑨	1.76%
Finance	$	95,000	1.90%
Other Operating	$	15,000	0.30%
Total Operating Expenses	$	2,098,000 ⑩	41.96%
EBIT (Earnings before Interest & Taxes)	$	102,000	2.04%
Interest Expenses	$	25,000	0.50%
EBT (Earnings before Taxes)	$	77,000	1.54%
Taxes	$	25,000	0.50%
Net Income (Earnings after Tax) ⑪	$	52,000	1.04%

Observed Analysis & Ratios *(Reference Numbers on P&L Above)*

1. **Sales to plan?** 95 %=($5.26M/ $5M). Sales fell short of budget by $260,000. This company needs to look for specific reasons why this occurred. Was the plan too ambitious? Were there operational factors that caused the target to be missed? What can be done differently in the future?

2. **Sales per square foot?** $200 = ($5M/25,000). This is a very average number in comparison to their retail sector. Comparable special order type operations selling medium to high end merchandise, have results in the $400 plus range. This company should investigate merchandising mix, traffic counts, and the effectiveness of its sales force. (This ratio varies across retail channels as seen in the approximate sales per square footage of 3 successful retailers: Wal-Mart: $430, Williams Sonoma: $1140, Apple: $6050.)

3. **Number of customers per salesperson per monthly average?** 193 = (18,519/12/8). This number indicates that the business is understaffed and can make improvements in sales management. Special order type operations that focus on matching the product to the customer with tools like project modeling, space planning, and concept design, operate in the area of 80-120 customers / salesperson / month. Too few salespeople for the customer count could alone be what caused sales to underperform to plan.

4. **Inventory to sales?** 20% = ($1M/ $5M). This business is on the verge of being over-inventoried. Comparable operations that are efficient will typically hold an average inventory of 15% of sales. That accounts for $250,000 less in stagnating asset purchases. Inefficiency also contributes to lower sales numbers and a higher expense structure. This company should implement better inventory management practices. Examples are open to buy purchasing systems, merchandising systems, and mark down systems.

5. **Gross margin is 44% of sales.** This company is outright throwing away 3-6 percentage points. This could be rectified through a variety of methods which may include: special order pricing guidelines; better and more creative price pointing; a quicker turning mark down system; variable commissions on gross margin; improving warranty protection plans and other product add-ons; more appropriate cost multipliers on vendors and categories; package and group pricing.

Underperforming margins are the easiest problem to fix unless the operation is extremely over inventoried (i.e. 25%+ Inventory/Sales).

6. The occupancy and advertising expense combined percent of sales? 15% = (8%+7%). Look at these two figures together because higher occupancy cost correlates positively with high traffic locations that require less advertising expense. Conversely, a destination location requires a greater advertising expense to pull people in. Whatever the situation, the combination of the two should not go above 15% of sales for this business. 15%+ can indicate that a retail operation is less viable, unless gross margins are very healthy – say 55%. This operation is on the cusp. Details of the rent paid to the owners and marketing expense need to be evaluated if this current sales level continues.

7. Are proper selling incentives and pay for performance programs in place? Salaries and commissions for sales staff are almost 9% of sales. This would be okay if the business was hitting sales targets and producing a nice bottom line. This business is not. The company should consider putting a selling incentive program in place that leads to higher margins and a faster turning inventory.

8. Service net percent of sales? 1%. This seems high. Are vendor credits getting processed? Perhaps there are excess damages because of higher inventory levels or some other operational issue. They should investigate.

9. Delivery/Shipping percent of sales? 1.76%. It's a good policy to offset delivery charges against delivery expenses. If this is being done, then the charges will sometimes cover the expenses. There may be opportunity of up to 1.5% in profit from the distribution department. This may be achieved through either charging proper setup and delivery fees or utilizing delivery staff and resources better.

10. Total operating costs as percent of sales? 41.96%. At 44% gross margin, this leaves only 2.04% in profitability before interest expense and taxes. That's not much to work with. 37% of sales is a total operating expense that comparable operations strive to achieve.

11. Earnings before taxes (EBT)? 1.54%. This is below average profitability. Growth will be difficult at this low level as there is only

$52,000 in cash that is generated from operations that will go into equity for the year after taxes are paid.

Consistently operating at this level can cause liquidity issues in the short term and solvency issues in the long run if there is ever a sudden economic down turn.

The numbers used in this article are similar to a real retailer. In the past year, I've seen businesses like this that have improved to double digit bottom lines before taxes.

You might ask, "So, what would happen to the bottom line of this company if the right improvements were made?"

Great question!

First, they need to be 100% committed and invest in the proper help. They could then improve their selling system to reach their sales target. They could take inventory management actions to get gross margin to 47%. As well, they could make slight adjustments to their merchandising, service, and delivery departments. Doing all this would produce an Earnings before Taxes of over 13%, or more than $700,000. The after tax net income would be close to 9%, or over $460,000!

That's why it is worth it to "Think Profit!"

24. THINK PROFIT!

Part 2 Balance Sheet Analysis

Most business managers can read a Profit and Loss Statement (P&L). Sales minus Merchandise Cost = Gross Margin minus Expenses = Income or Loss, right? This is what people easily understand and focus on. The two other critical financial reports, the Balance Sheet and the Statement of Cash Flow are often ignored or are improperly analyzed. In my previous writing, I covered the basics of analyzing a Profit and Loss Statement. In this writing, I extend my analysis and case study to the Balance Sheet.

The Balance Sheet is also known as the Statement of Financial Position. This is because it is a snapshot at one "position" in time, usually at a period end. It started when you first opened your business, and does not end until your business is either done or sold. In contrast, the Profit and Loss Statement represents a range in time and is reset to zero each year. When the P&L is reset, your income or loss for that year is recorded as equity in your Balance Sheet's Retained Earnings account each year. If you have successive years of large profits, your equity in your business grows. The equity that you retain in the business is what helps finance the business. It is what fuels growth, longevity, and business health.

Analyzing your Balance Sheet is critical because it shows the ability of your business to remain in business. It highlights the strengths and weaknesses of your financial position. The way this is accomplished is through ratio analysis. A ratio is the result of comparing two different numbers. It is a point of measurement. Once you calculate important ratios for your business, comparisons can be made with industry averages, peer performance groups, or historical results. By doing this, you can identify areas to focus on and rate your improvement actions.

Case Study

Following is the Balance Sheet. It is a common sized statement. That means that alongside each dollar figure is the percentage of total assets that number represents. These percentages enable companies like this to compare themselves with their industry. It makes businesses of different sizes common, so they can be compared against each other. I have also included a comparative column so that we can see the change from the previous year.

Company Background

- Independently owned and operated.
- One store operation with one detached warehouse.
- Shareholders own the buildings separately and the business pays them rent.
- 25,000 square foot showroom.
- Vendor merchandising = mid to upper.
- Special order percentage = 50%.
- Sales for year ended = $5,000,000.
- Cost of Goods Sold = $2,800,000 @ 56%.
- Gross Margin = $2,200,000 @ 44%.
- Net Income before tax = 1.54%
- Net Income after Interest and Tax = $52,000 @ 1.04%.

Balance Sheet (Statement of Financial Position)

	Dec. 31, 20XX	% of Assets	Prior Year Comparative	% of Assets
Current Assets				
Cash	$165,000	11%	$210,000	15%
Marketable Securities ❺❻	$50,000	3%	$65,000	4%
Accounts Receivable	$100,000	7%	$75,000	5%
Inventory ❼❽❾	$1,025,000	71%	$975,000	67%
Prepaid Expenses	$10,000	1%	$10,000	1%
Total Current Assets ❸❹	$1,350,000	93%	$1,335,000	92%
Long-term Assets: ❶				
Property, Plant, & Equipment (Net)	$100,000	7%	$110,000	8%
Total Long-term Assets	$100,000	7%	$110,000	8%
Total Assets ❿	**$1,450,000**	100%	**$1,445,000**	100%
Current Liabilities:				
Accounts Payable	$250,000	17%	$240,000	17%
Salaries Payable	$25,000	2%	$20,000	1%
Taxes Payable	$20,000	1%	$20,000	1%
Customer Deposits	$550,000	38%	$600,000	42%
Line of Credit	$50,000	3%	$37,000	3%
Notes Payable	$25,000	2%	$25,000	2%
Total Current Liabilities ❸❹	$920,000	63.45%	$942,000	65%
Long-term Liabilities:				
Notes Payable - bank	$350,000	24%	$375,000	26%
Total Long-term Liabilities	$350,000	24.14%	$375,000	26%
Total Liabilities ❷	$1,270,000	87.59%	$1,317,000	91.14%
Stockholder's Equity:				
Retained Earnings	$103,000	7%	$73,000	5%
Net Income (loss) Year to Date ❿⓫	$52,000	4%	$30,000	2%
Paid in Capital	$25,000	2%	$25,000	2%
Total Stockholder's Equity ⓫	$180,000	12.41%	$128,000	8.86%
Total Liabilities and Stockholder's Equity	**$1,450,000**	100%	**$1,445,000**	100%

Note: *Select Ratios reference the circled numbers on the sample Balance Sheet.*

(1) Where are the assets? 93% of their assets are current. Current means that the assets are expected to be converted into cash in less than one year. Long term assets represent only 7% of total assets. This is probably due to the fact that the owners own the buildings separately and they are paying themselves rent. This is common. This company's health could be improved by reducing the weight of assets in inventory and accounts receivable vs. assets held in cash and securities. It would be more secure to see 18-20% of total assets in Cash and Securities.

(2) How are the assets financed? This can be seen in the percent of total assets under liabilities and equity. This business is 12% internally financed and 88% debt financed. Their financing comes from three sources for the most part: their vendors, their customers, and their bank.

(3) Net Working Capital (WC) $430,000. (= Current Assets − Current Liabilities.) It represents a company's ability to pay off its short-term debt. This business seems OK when looking at working capital as a dollar amount. In cases where working capital is negative, the business will have difficulty meeting its obligations. Negative WC is the definition of insolvency. That would be a precursor to liquidation.

(4) Current Ratio 1.47. (= Current Assets / Current Liabilities.) Current ratio is a measure of liquidity. It gives a comparable picture of business health as opposed to net working capital because it can be applied to businesses of all sizes. Although some industries are different than others, a current ratio of a 2 or 2:1 is considered decent. A current ratio of 1 would mean that the business can just cover its debt if it became due. Here a 1.47 clearly shows there is room for improvement.

(5) Quick Ratio .34. (= (Cash + Mkt. Securities + AR) / Current Liabilities.) Quick Ratio is a more conservative measure of liquidity. Inventory is a much less liquid asset, so it is removed from the equation. A Quick Ratio of .5 is considered in this industry to be decent. A .34 could be from either an inventory or debt level that is too large for its size.

(6) Cash Ratio 23%. (= (Cash + Market Securities) / Current Liabilities.) Cash ratio is an even more conservative liquidity measure. Over 25% is good. Also note that the comparative cash balance from the prior year to the year ended fell by around 20%.

(7) Inventory Turnover 2.8 times. (= Cost of Goods (annualized) / Average Inventory.) One reason why this business is not as liquid as it could be shows itself here. Turns are lower than their average industry peers are getting. A slower inventory translates itself into higher liabilities and lower cash flow.

(8) Days Sales in Inventory 130 days. (= 365 days / Turns.) On average, it takes this business 130 days to sell and deliver a piece of merchandise. That's tough when they have to pay most vendors in 30 days. Top operations are turning in less than 100 days. And a few retailers turn so fast, and their terms are so good, that areas of their inventory are fully vendor financed.

(9) Gross Margin Return on Inventory (GMROI) is $2.20. (= Gross Margin Dollars (annualized) / Average Inventory.) $2.20 certainly is not bad. But it's not great either. GMROI is the ultimate gauge of Return on Investment efficiency with inventory operations. Most high profit operations live above $2.50.

(10) Return on Assets (ROA) 4%. (= Net income / Average Total Assets.) Like GMROI, ROA is a return ratio. This, however, compares the net income produced by the assets invested. This is one of the most telling signs of this company's below average results in profitability. Average total assets of over $1.4 million only produced $52,000 in after tax income last year. ROA should be above 20%. A company I recently worked with had achieved almost 50% ROA!

(11) Return on Equity (ROE) 34%. (= Net Income / Average Total Equity.) Equity for the most part is what ownership puts into the business and the profits it leaves there. It is either shareholder debt or equity that enables a business to operate and purchase and sell its assets (its inventory). Unless investors inject a continuous stream of cash, equity usually comes from net income. A 34% ratio is on the low side. It could be due to the company being a new business, or the shareholders taking out profits, or in this case, it is the lack of successive high profit years. If this business takes the right actions to become a high profit operation, puts some profits back in the business, and uses its capital properly, the equity will assist their growth. As it does, its Balance Sheet will strengthen and its future will become brighter.

Conclusion

The company in this example has much room for improvement. The analysis of their P&L and then their Balance Sheet indicates that they should focus on improving some specific areas of their inventory and sales management.

They can adopt an overall goal and implement a strategy to raise GMROI from $2.20 to $2.60… just 40 cents. They can take steps to improve their overall profitability. I would also advise that they reinvest some equity in the business to fund growth.

"Well, 40 cents in GMROI improvement doesn't sound like that much. What would be the effect," you might ask.

Great question!

Right, 40 cents does not sound like much. Think of it this way: at $1 Million in average inventory, if this operation had 40 cents extra in GMROI, that would equate to $400,000 in extra Gross Margin dollars generated each year! Their financial position would become much more lucrative.

That's why it is worth it to Think Profit!

25. THINK PROFIT!

Part 3 Cash Flow Analysis

Proper cash levels enable businesses to continue operations. With adequate cash, inventories can be kept at the correct levels, employees can be hired and paid properly, and capital reinvestment becomes possible. Without cash, extra financing may be required through delayed vendor payments or loans. Additional interest could be incurred. If cash levels get too low, vendor shipments could be slowed and the businesses may eventually become insolvent.

Cash comes from profit. How funds are used, ultimately determines the level of liquidity and the ending cash available in a retail business. Well-run operations have consistently adequate net income levels. They also have proper budgets to control the levels of major cash usage accounts: inventory, accounts payable, deposits, and receivables. Well-run firms exhibit high levels of stability – in ALL economies. That allows for self-investment, which leads to growth and even greater levels of prosperity.

Alternatively, operations that don't understand how cash is REALLY accumulated, often experience cash shortages. They have higher debt levels. Coincidentally, poor performing operations are often the ones that have very tight expense controls and loose balance sheet controls at the same time. Well run operations can afford to spend money on what counts **BECAUSE they ARE well run operations**.

Poorly managed retailers just can't afford it. Some operations that are profitable on their P&L's due to being "excruciatingly frugal", are unguided when it comes to inventory, payables, and deposits/receivables. This is a situation that can lead profitable companies to insolvency. Some are eventually forced into bankruptcy.

If you feel in the dark at times as to why your cash is at the level it is, this writing is for you. Here, I build upon the case scenario in my previous 2 writings.

To start, here is a simplified equation for cash:

> **Beginning cash + net profit - increase in assets - decrease in liabilities = Ending cash.**

To illustrate this:

What would happen to cash if: net income was $100,000 and inventory went up by $50,000 and Accounts Payable went up by $75,000?

Profit brings in $100k cash, inventory uses $50K, and there was a supplier loan increase of $75k. Cash would have gone up by $125,000.

Wouldn't it be great if you could see this information clearly every month and even project into the future? Well, if you have proper financial statements and know how to use them, you already have this information. It is one of your most important management reports. It is your Statement of Cash Flow.

I'm often curious. Why do many business owners avoid one of their most important management reports? The only answers that I can come up with are that either they don't have the proper monthly financial reporting procedures or that they simply don't understand. And, if they don't understand, they can't have a properly functioning financial system. The third, kind of scary answer, is that they don't believe the Statement of Cash Flow is important.

If you are reading this, you care.

In an effort to increase knowledge of how to use a Statement of Cash Flow, let's consider the following scenario:

Company Background

- Independently owned and operated.
- One store operation with one detached warehouse.
- The shareholders own the buildings separately and the business pays them rent.
- 25,000 square foot showroom.
- Eight salespeople, one sales manager.
- Average sale = $1,350; traffic count for the year ended = 18,519; close rate = 20%.
- $1,000,000 average inventory at cost.
- Vendor merchandising – mid to upper end.
- Special order percentage = 50%.
- Budgeted sales were $5.26 Million.
- Sales for the year ended = $5,000,000.
- Cost of Goods Sold = $2,800,000 @ 56%.
- Gross Margin = $2,200,000 @ 44%.
- Net Income after Interest and Tax = $52,000 @ 1.04%.

Statement of Cash Flow for Year End

Dec. 31, 20XX

Cash Flow from Operations		
Net Earnings (loss)	❶	52000
Additions (subtractions) to Cash		
Depreciation Addition	❷	10000
Changes in Accounts Receivable	❸	-25000
Changes in Inventory	❹	-50000
Changes in Accounts Payable	❺	10000
Changes in Salaries Payable	❻	5000
Changes in Customer Deposits	❼	-50000
Changes in Line of Credit	❽	13000
Total Cash From Operating Activities	❾	**-87000**
Cash Flow from Investing Activities		
Capital Expeditures, PPE		0
Total Cash Flows from Investing Activities	❿	0
Cash Flow from Financing Activities		
Dividends Paid		
Sale, Purchase of Stock		
Net Borrowings, LT Notes		-25000
Total Cash Flow form Financing Activities	⓫	**-25000**
Change in Cash flow and Cash Equivilants	⓬	**-60000**
Add Begginning Cash Flow	⓭	**275000**
Cash Ending Balance Dec. 31, 2011	⓮	**215000**

Note: the below numbers refer to the circled numbers in the Cash Flow Statement.

(1) Net income: Inflow of cash for this retailer is $52,000. It had $5 million in sales, 44% Gross Margin, approximately 42% in operating costs, and the net income after tax as a percent of sales was 1.04%. This retailer only has $52,000 going into cash flow from profit. This alone does not determine the ending cash flow. Transactions that are not sales and expense related now come into play.

(2) Depreciation: In addition to profit and loss activity, other regular business operating activities affect whether cash goes up or down. These non P&L activities occur on the balance sheet. They affect cash flow just the same. The first one, depreciation, is listed as an addition to cash purely because it was already recorded as a reduction against net income (and it really did not affect cash as it is a non-cash expense). In this example, a $10,000 addition to cash is recorded due to depreciation. A side note here: it is important to keep up with your depreciation schedule on a monthly basis rather than in one chunk at the end of the year to get a better idea of your profitability throughout the year.

(3) Changes in receivables: Outflow $25,000 cash. Cash went down because receivables increased during the year. In other words, this business lent customers a net of $25,000 rather than collecting at the time of the delivered sale.

(4) Changes in inventory: Outflow $50,000 cash. They ended up carrying $50,000 more in inventory during the period. Inventory has very important effects on cash, seen on both the balance sheet in terms of purchases, and on the income statement in terms of carrying costs. You can't live with it and you can't live without it. This firm has a 20% inventory to sales ratio. This is too much considering they were short of their sales plan.

(5) Changes to accounts payable: Inflow of cash $10,000. Consider payables as a short term (often interest free) trade loan. If you hold more payables, you have a larger loan since you have paid out less cash. The trick here is to find your balance between getting

David W. McMahon, CMA

this interest free loan, considering the value of taking any trade discounts, and avoiding becoming late on accounts that could affect your services, credit rating, or inventory flow.

(6) Changes in Salaries payable: Inflow of cash $5,000. This company brought on a couple of new employees at the end of the year causing salaries owing to increase for the prior year final period. In other words – they have a temporary loan from unpaid wages.

(7) Changes in Customer deposits: Outflow $50,000 cash. They took in fewer deposits on special order sales. This figure is a concern and should be investigated. Was the decrease in deposits due to a decrease in written sales? Was it due to salespeople not following the policy of asking for full payment and getting a 50% deposit minimum? Or, was it from a decline in special order sales vs. sales from stock. Whatever the reasons, wouldn't you want to know why, if it were your business?

(8) Changes in the Line of Credit: Inflow of cash $13,000. Ok, I'll throw this out there now: not all reasons for additions to cash are good reasons. Store management decided to dig into their line of credit (LOC) at the end of the year to fund a new container shipment. Their LOC loan went up resulting in a cash increase. Using a credit line could be good or bad depending on the reason. Here this retailer is over-inventoried. They clearly should not have invested in new, untested merchandise which could result in ongoing cash flow shortfalls.

(9) Total cash flows from operating activities: Outflow $87,000 cash. So here we have the case of a profitable company actually losing money! By looking only at the P&L, an *uninformed* analyst could draw the conclusion that they are breaking even so – no worries on the cash side. By looking only at the balance sheet, an *uniformed* analyst may conclude that they have a sustainable cash balance so – they are good. But by looking at the statement of cash flow, where both the results of the P&L and the Balance Sheet are represented, the ***informed*** analyst can provide the proper advice – they have a cash burn rather than cash earn. It's a situation that can be of concern or not, depending on the underlying reasons.

156

(10) Cash flow from investing activities: No cash flow effect. Investing activities are different than operating activities as they typically take the form of capital expenditures and longer term fixed asset purchases. For example, if the company were to purchase new equipment or machinery for its distribution center, the value of that equipment purchase would cause a cash decrease. If the reinvestment is for business improvements, the goal is to gain a greater return on the investment and a subsequent increase in cash flow in regular operating income. Reinvestments are important in developing innovations for new revenue streams or increases in efficiencies. This company did not engage in any investing activities during the past year.

(11) Cash flow from financing activities: The outflow is $25,000 cash. Financing activities are the last category, after operating and investing activities, on the cash flow statement. In this section we can observe cash effects due to activities that support the long term funding of a business, as well as any effects of the sale of company stock or payment of dividends. In this scenario, the only effect was due to a decrease in the long term note on the business.

(12) Change in cash flow: Outflow of $60,000. This is the net cash flow result for the year. Again, even though this retailer made $52,000 after sales and expenses, it lost $60,000 in cash. That's a $112,000 difference. If the cash had been spent as an appropriate reinvestment with a plan that might be ok. In this scenario, I believe the operation did not have the knowledge or strategy in place. They never consistently reviewed their key performance indicators (KPIs).

(13) Beginning cash: Cash at the start of the period was $275,000.

(14) Ending cash: Cash at the end of the period is $215,000. ($275,000 – $60,000).

Conclusion & Recommendations

This case study is based on an actual retail company I worked with closely. They were in fairly rough shape. However, we were able to focus their management team on improving their business. As of this publishing, they are hitting their sales goals. They are managing their inventory supply chain professionally. And, they are approaching double digit net income.

Here is a summary key observations and action items that I gave prior to their turn around.

Observations:

- Sales goals were missed due to a variety of sales management issues.
- Inventory levels are too high for the sales volume.
- Gross margin is underperforming.

Action Items:

- Establish professional financial projections under alternate scenarios that help guide business strategy.
- Hire and properly train 2 or 3 new salespeople.
- Improve the effectiveness of the customer relationship management system (CRM). Manage it.
- Focus on better customer follow up. Track it.
- Increase average sales through new warranty programs. Track them.
- Improve inventory management systems and closely watch key performance indicators.
- Establish open to buy guidelines for purchases of new merchandise.
- Develop the Head Buyers abilities.
- Price special orders and best sellers appropriately. I.e. 2.5 over landed as a guide.
- Implement a system to properly price point merchandise.
- Religious execution of price markdown strategy to identify and sell dead merchandise.

Final Result

Oh – you might ask how much this company's profits and cash flow increased as a result of these changes.

Great question!

The results for their last year end were are a 470% increase in profitability. They produced an after tax net income increase of over $245,000. Cash flow increased by over 130% to $513,000 from $215,000.

That is why it is essential to take action based on a careful review of your three major financial statements:

- Your P&L
- Your Balance Sheet
- Your Statement of Cash Flow

THINK PROFIT!

26. CASH FLOW RED FLAGS

How could this happen?

It must have been the economy!

Let me tell you the story of a business that was founded over 50 years ago. They had grown from a small mom and pop shop to an organization that operated three stores and did $10 million+ in sales. Times were good—for a while. Then recently, they declared bankruptcy and closed their doors.

A slow economy, as in many cases like this, was only one factor. In fact, in this case there was only a modest decline in revenue relative to similar businesses in the region. The primary factor for their demise was an outright failure to be a student of their business.

Their family had grown so there were more people to support. Between the various brothers, sisters, sons, daughters, and cousins, there were multiple people who relied on the business to pay for their mortgages and feed their families. On top of this, there was no clear leader. Every decision had to go through a sort of unanimous voting process. This slowed their speed to react and innovate. The decisions that were made were often times on issues that were not of any great benefit to the business.

They wasted time. It got so bad that there was one petty argument that I witnessed, amongst the "managers", on who was supposed to put the toilet paper in the bathrooms! They had little time left to focus on what counted. The family ownership was really challenged with professional managerial focus.

They were just concerned with written sales. They ignored all the other business signs or did not know where to look for them. They thought, "There will be cash to pay the bills, if we have a good sales weekend, right?" Yeah – right…

Eventually they decided to take a loan to refinance their growing accounts payable. They used debt to pay for their debt. They tried mass event sales to blow out their inventory. They were just able to break even. They repeated this act of refinancing and big event sales. Eventually they became insolvent. This meant that they could not pay for their short term obligations. Minimal profitability, missing sales goals, and rising debt put the nail in their coffin. **Bankrupt.**

Unfortunately, stories like this are far too common. This company needed a responsible leader. If they had a leader that built a team who knew which red flags to look for and took decisive actions sooner, they may have survived.

In this writing, I'm going to show you the red flags to look for. If you keep your eyes on these flags, you will greatly improve your chances of success. You will be able to take corrective measures sooner. With you, as the decisive leader of your capable team, your cash flow potential can be realized.

Red Flag 1: Sales to Plan

Sales drive everything. Your plan is your realistic projection. It is your budget. The sales plan is the dollar amount needed to produce your required profitability and cash flow. For example, if sales were $550,000 and planned sales were $525,000, then sales to plan is 105 percent ($550K/$525K). Great. Anything over 100% exceeds the goal. Anything under is a miss.

Sales to Plan should be checked monthly, quarterly, and year-to-date. Repeated underperformance of sales to plan signifies either performance issues with sales or a budget that needs to be rethought.

Red Flag 2: Profitability (a.ka. Net Income)

Profitability or net income is the ultimate source of all business sustainable cash flow. It is sales minus all your expenses. To view as a percent, divide net income by sales. No operation can operate with a loss for very long. Few can operate at average profitability (2-4 percent) and have ample funds to grow their business. There is just too much pressure on making regular short-term payables, which can fluctuate.

Alternatively, healthy profitability (7 percent+) enables growth through reinvestment of equity into the business. This investment leads to expansion and takes the form of technology, training, capital investment, merchandise lines, and human talent. Paying out all the profit to shareholders does little for the future of business. It is important to note that profitability needs to be consistent to really make a difference. Check your net profit percent every month on certifiably correct financial statements for month-end and year-to-date.

Red Flag 3: Quick Ratio

Also called the acid test ratio, quick ratio is a measure of the liquidity that you have in your business. It is calculated by taking your current assets, less your inventory divided by your current liabilities. Current assets are assets that can be converted into cash in under 1 year. Current liabilities are debts that are due in under 1 year. An even quick ratio of 1 is good in many retail sectors. Anything under .5 may indicate a danger area. Companies with very low quick ratios are at risk of insolvency.

Red Flag 4: Cash to Current Payables

Cash to current payables measures your ability to pay for your immediate vendor responsibilities. It largely indicates whether you can honor your short term loans from your vendors. It is critical to continue uninterrupted flow of goods. I have seen some companies that have shut their doors because their vendors simply stopped shipping to them. Alternatively, I have seen companies with $0 payables. In any effect, try to keep cash / payables consistently above 25%. Businesses under 15% may struggle to make ends meet and are more likely to dip into lines of credit.

Red Flag 5: GMROI

Gross margin return on inventory. All your cash comes from selling inventory and services, right? If you sell your inventory faster or carry less of it, you generate cash faster, right? That's what GMROI is—the ultimate measure of your operations effectiveness at creating dollars! Figure this by annualizing your gross margin dollars and dividing by your average or current inventory on hand. Do it every month without fail. Seek to continually improve this number overall. I call a $2 GMROI a break-even GMROI and a $2.5+ GMROI an "in the money" GMROI. (This varies between retail merchandise categories.)

Red Flag 6: Inventory to Sales

Inventory to sales is your red flag for new buying. Purchasing should follow sales results or realistic forecasts. You all know what could happen if you go to a trade show and you buy without a plan. Only a certain percent of the new merchandise that you purchase, sells; the rest sits in stagnation. Obviously, invoices become due for that inventory whether it sells or not. Your timing and the amount you spend on new merchandise is everything. In fact, most of the businesses that I have seen go bust were overbought. Figure your inventory to sales by taking your average or current inventory that is in your possession and divide it by your annualized sales. I call 14-17% the "sweet spot" for some. In fast turning retail sectors, I see under 8% inventory to sales. Only purchase new merchandise if your inventory to sales ratio is in your "sweet spot" range.

Red Flag 7: Gross Margin

How much money do you have left to pay for all operating costs and make a healthy profit after you deduct your cost of goods and freight from the sale of your merchandise? That is your gross margin. Figure as a percent each month and year-to-date by dividing by gross margin dollars by sales dollars.

Small and medium volume retailers have few economies of scale. So, they need gross margin to live. Fixed operating costs can eat profits unless margins are appropriate. Unless you have a killer deal on rent and a great location, a store doing under $5 million will find it difficult to operate at under 45 percent margin overall.

Alternatively, for example, a store with sales of over $20 million could operate at a lower margin and be a low cost seller and still be decently profitable. Turns make up for lower gross margins.

Below is a profit matrix showing where cash is typically made with respect to gross margin and turns. Avoid the "death zone".

PROFIT MATRIX	Low Gross Margin	High Gross Margin
High Turns	"Profit Potential"	"Huge Profit!"
Low Turns	"Death Zone"	"Profit Potential"

Red Flag 8: Operating Cost Ratio

Operating costs are all the costs that you incur each month after your landed cost of goods are deducted. You should set target percentages of sales by department in your master budget so that you can avoid expense-profit erosion. Commonly tracked departments in retail operating budgets are: administration, occupancy, selling, marketing, service, warehouse, delivery, and finance. Note that payroll should be separated by their respective department. Many high profit retailer operations that I work with seek to be under 37% in total operating cost as a percent of sales.

Whatever your market segment, be a student of your business. Watch for your red flags. This is a major step on your road to achieving a healthier cash flow position. Being in-tune gives you longevity whatever your sales volume is. The next step is to take the right decisive actions at the right time.

"If you measure it, you CAN improve it!"

27. RETAIL BREAK EVEN ANALYSIS

Lower your breakeven point and make money sooner

During the great recession, high exposure to risk forced many retailers to go out of business. The culprit commonly was high fixed costs relative to total costs. When consumer spending suddenly slowed, businesses were unable to respond in time to the sales downturn. These retailers simply fell uncontrollably and quickly beneath their break-even points of sales. Losses were incurred, and eventually their cash flow dried up.

Of course there were those that did survive the recession and remain profitable. Typically they had a greater proportion of variable costs (lower fixed costs). Due to this, they shouldered less risk. You see, businesses with more variable costs in lieu of fixed costs are less susceptible to sudden changes in sales volume. Variable costs rise and fall in proportion to sales and result in a lower break-even point of sales. This gives these stores an advantage over their competition. There is more time, or room, before cash reserves are depleted during a sudden sales slump.

In this writing I will demonstrate how to calculate your break-even point of sales. I will also provide some real world examples of ways smart retailers reduce their break-even points. So, what is the formula for break-even sales?

First, you need to have a clear definition of Fixed and Variable costs:

Fixed costs: These are costs that do not change when sales fluctuate. Examples are administrative costs, rent, and fixed salaries.

Variable costs: costs that go up and down with sales. Examples are cost of goods sold, sales commissions, finance company fees, and credit card fees.

What complicates the retail costing environment are the mixed costs. They are a mix between fixed and variable costs. Examples could be: advertising costs, distribution costs, and customer service costs. To get a firm grasp on how mixed costs affect your business you need to ask yourself: if sales go up or down... does this cost stay the same and, if not, how much does it fluctuate?

Calculating Break-even

Once you have a good grasp of your cost types, you can calculate your contribution margin ratio. This is the point where fixed costs are covered. Any sales dollars that are above that level contribute to profits at your contribution margin rate.

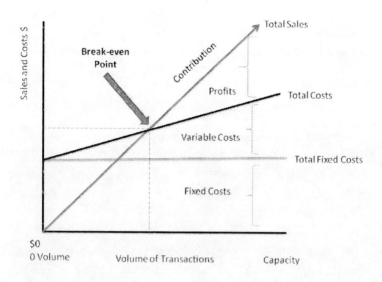

Contribution margin % = (Sales – Variable Costs) / Sales

Let's use the real life example of a store we will call XYZ Stores. This retailer has sales of $6,000,000, variable costs of $3,800,000 and fixed costs of $1,500,000.

Contribution margin % = ($6,000,000 - $3,800,000) / $6,000,000 = 36.667%.

What does a contribution margin ratio of 36.667% mean? It means that after fixed costs are covered, 36.667% of any sale is straight profit. So, once you know your fixed costs, variable costs, and contribution margin you can easily figure your break-even point of sales.

In the example, the retail break-even for XYZ Stores is:

> **Break-even Sales = Fixed Costs/Contribution Margin %**

= $1,500,000/36.667% = $4,090,909

Break-even Analysis
XYZ Stores vs. Peer Comparison

	XYZ Stores	% of Sales	High Profit Peers	% of Sales	Average Peers	% of Sales
Sales	$ 6,000,000	100%	$6,000,000	100%	$6,000,000	100%
Cost of Goods	$ 3,300,000	55.00%	$3,270,000	54.50%	$3,366,000	56.10%
Gross Margin	$ 2,700,000	45.00%	$2,730,000	45.50%	$2,634,000	43.90%
Variable Operating Expenses	$ 500,000	8.33%	$ 654,000	10.90%	$ 688,200	11.47%
Contribution Margin	$ 2,200,000	36.67%	$2,076,000	34.60%	$1,945,800	32.43%
Fixed Expenses	$ 1,500,000	25.00%	$1,722,000	28.70%	$1,837,800	30.63%
Net Profit	$ 700,000	11.67%	$ 354,000	5.90%	$ 108,000	1.80%
Break-even Sales	$ 4,090,909		$4,976,879		$5,666,975	
Break-even Sales/Month	$ 340,909		$ 414,740		$ 472,248	

This company needs to reach $4,090,909 in sales before it makes 1 cent in profit out of total sales of $6,000,000. This is where the old saying that "Retailers don't make 1 cent until black Friday" comes from.

Black Friday is a myth. We all know that the term is only used in a metaphorical way when thinking of a calendar year. Profit is made each and every day once you crest your daily break-even point. But due to the weekends being responsible for the "lion's share" of retail volume, you should express your break-even as a monthly and/or weekly sales threshold. (If you wish, you can consider the number of weekend days in the month as well.)

The monthly break-even sales level for XYZ Stores is $4,090,909/12 =$340,909 (without seasonal fluctuations). This is the minimum sales volume that adds to cash rather than subtracts from it.

Reducing Break-even Point

Now that you are tracking break-even properly, you CAN improve it.

It's never too late to switch fixed expenses to a variable structure or transition to a greater variable proportion of mixed expenses. This will reduce your risk exposure (financial leverage) and maximize your cash flow over the years.

Listed below are some real world examples of how smart retailers are reducing their break-even:

- Use a Contribution Margin Financial Statement so you can easily calculate your break-even every month. This consistent tracking enables you to react FAST.

- Focus on margins.

- Increase availability of warranty programs. If a dealer increases GM, their BE falls. Warranty is a fast way to increase GM$ because when sales go up, Cost of Goods Sold goes down, and BE decreases as profit increases.

- Offer various financing options.

- Use variable sliding sales commissions based on gross margin percent.

- Pay the delivery crews by the stops or piece numbers rather than on salary.

- Set departmental budgets based on sales volume levels rather than just expense levels: administrative, warehouse, and advertising.

- Renegotiate rent, if possible, as a percent of sales rather than fixed cost.

- Set inventory levels that are based on sales levels to incur variable carrying costs.

- Track return on advertising dollars more closely with respect to selling opportunities and traffic online and offline.

- Employ efficient systems, procedures, and equipment in business operations.

- Develop effective and fair vendor credit programs.

- Pay managers and owners as a percent of sales and profitability rather than just straight salary.

- Invest in advice and training that impacts profitability and improves sales.

Now that you have some practices that will improve break-even sales, what results can you expect?

Please refer to the previous spreadsheet. Again, XYZ Stores is generating $6,000,000 in annual sales.

First let's figure net income using the formula: Net income = Sales − Variable Costs − Fixed expenses.

In this example, the company has a net income of $700,000 per year = $6,000,000-$3,800,000-$1,500,000.

That's almost a 12% net profit margin ($700,000 / $6,000,000 = 11.67%). This resembles a real retail client who accomplished this.

Here is a little bonus calculation for you. What if you have done everything you possibly could? You have established the lowest break-even possible with your individual circumstances. Now, you want to figure out how to prosper further. How many extra sales dollars do you need to produce your desired profitability and subsequent increase in cash flow?

Let's use our example of XYZ Stores whose management team asked, "We want to be able to get our profitability up by an extra $100,000 this year. Although we continually seek to improve our break-even we feel that we have an efficient and effective structure in place. What sales increase do we need to get that extra $100,000 in profit?"

I responded, "Your sales last year were $6,000,000 and you produced $700,000 in net income. All we need to do is take your fixed costs, add in your desired operating income and divide by your contribution margin %."

This was all done in seconds from their contribution margin financial statement.

I added, "If your contribution margin remains constant, you will only need sales of $6,272,157 ($1,500,000 + $800,000 / 36.67%). $272,157 sales dollars would make you an extra $100,000 in profit. That is just an increase of $22,680 in sales per month."

Sales for desired profit = (FC + Desired Profit) / CM%

"Based on the sales equation of Average Sale x Traffic x Close Rate, that's really not too many more repeat customers or visitors on the web site each month.", I informed them.

We all agreed that with proper management, training, and execution an extra $100,000 was possible!

The lesson here: Think PROFIT first, then translate that to SALES.

28. FLEXIBLE BUDGETING

We have all heard the saying, "A failure to plan, is a plan to fail." Most independent retailers don't have an actionable plan. I did say most. The best operators do plan. They use forecasts and budgets to help them react faster to unforeseen situations in the future. A quantifiable plan is a budget.

To introduce you to the value of budgeting, in this writing I will show you how you can use a simplified "Flexible Budget" to assist with your operational forecasting.

This process is called "Flexible" because your planned level of sales may change due to unforeseen factors. For example, if your local economy is dominated by a large employer that suddenly lays off half of its work force, there may be a spillover effect on your business. Flexible budgeting allows you to prepare better for the unknown.

Flexible Budgeting lets you "Flex" your top line and observe the resulting operational effects on your P&L and operating income. To see these effects, a non-traditional financial statement will be used that separates variable expenses and fixed expenses. This is called a contribution margin financial statement and can be used for internal reporting, planning and analysis. The separation of variable and fixed expenses is important because they act differently when sales volume changes.

Examples of variable costs in the retail environment are cost of goods sold, sales commissions, finance company fees, and a portion of marketing and distribution costs. These expenses are only incurred when a sale is made. When you look at total variable costs, you see that as output (sales) increases, variable costs increase at the same rate. If you look at variable costs per unit of output, they remain fairly constant. For example, the ratio of sales commissions to sales may be 7% no matter what the output volume is.

The behavior of fixed expenses on the other hand is different. Total fixed costs will remain the same on a dollar amount over the relevant range of activity. For example, if rent is $30,000 per month, it's going to be $30,000 per month whatever your output volume is, provided you're in business. Conversely, fixed costs per unit of output decline as output increases. So, if your sales levels increase, you pay less as a percentage of sales. The spread of the increase or decrease directly adds or takes away from bottom line profitability. This is economies of scale.

Example of Cost Behavior:

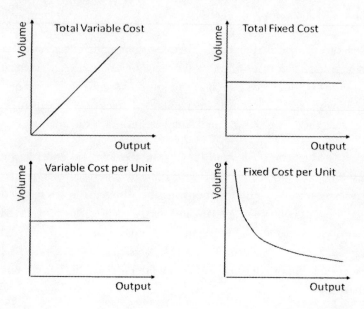

Contribution Margin Financial Statement and Flexible Budget Example:

	Master or Static Budget		Flexible Budget		Flexible Budget	
	Sales $ Flexed at:	100%	Sales $ Flexed at:	90%	Sales $ Flexed at:	110%
Sales	$ 500,000	100%	$ 450,000	100%	$ 550,000	100%
Less Variable Expenses						
Cost of Goods Sold	$ 260,000	52.0%	$ 234,000	52.0%	$ 286,000	52.0%
Gross Margin	$ 240,000	48.0%	$ 216,000	48.0%	$ 264,000	48.0%
Sales Commissions	$ 35,000	7.0%	$ 31,500	7.0%	$ 38,500	7.0%
Other Variable	$ 10,000	2.0%	$ 9,000	2.0%	$ 11,000	2.0%
Total Variable Expenses	$ 305,000	61.0%	$ 274,500	61.0%	$ 335,500	61.0%
Contribution Margin	$ 195,000	39.0%	$ 175,500	39.0%	$ 214,500	39.0%
Less Fixed Expenses						
Administration Expenses	$ 100,000	20.0%	$ 100,000	22.2%	$ 100,000	18.2%
Occupancy Expenses	$ 30,000	6.0%	$ 30,000	6.7%	$ 30,000	5.5%
Marketing Expense (Fixed Portion)	$ 25,000	5.0%	$ 25,000	5.6%	$ 25,000	4.5%
Selling Expense (Fixed Portion)	$ 1,000	0.2%	$ 1,000	0.2%	$ 1,000	0.2%
Distribution Expense (Fixed Portion)	$ 15,000	3.0%	$ 15,000	3.3%	$ 15,000	2.7%
Other Fixed Expenses	$ 5,000	1.0%	$ 5,000	1.1%	$ 5,000	0.9%
Total Fixed Expenses	$ 176,000	35.2%	$ 176,000	39.1%	$ 176,000	32.0%
Operating Income	$ 19,000	3.8%	$ (500)	-0.1%	$ 38,500	7.0%
Break Even Sales	$ 451,282		$ 451,282		$ 451,282	

The place to start is with your actual financial statements that you produce in your software system. From your P&L, identify which balances are variable expenses, which are fixed, and which are mixed. From there you can use a spreadsheet to create a contribution margin financial statement similar to the one shown above.

Enter your master budget numbers. This is your most likely scenario. In the example, monthly sales are targeted at $500,000. It's also important to note here that many businesses experience seasonality, so master budget sales numbers often should differ from month to month. After sales come variable expenses. Start with cost of goods sold as that is the largest variable component in retail. From there you can see your target gross margin. After gross margin, enter your other common variable expenses such as commissions. Here I lumped all the other variable costs in one category. You can separate the individual costs out if you deem them to be of material importance.

Subtracting total variable expenses from sales gives you your contribution margin dollars and contribution margin ratio as a percent of sales. Contribution margin percent shows the percentage added to net income once fixed expenses are covered. So here, once the business is over break even, every $1 increase in sales adds $.39 to operating income.

After contribution margin, all fixed expenses should be subtracted. This results in the net operating income for the month's sales.

If you are creating a contribution margin statement, take the next small step and figure your break even. In my writing on Retail Break-even, I explained the formula as: Fixed Expenses divided by Contribution Margin Ratio.

(Note: You cannot figure your breakeven properly without a contribution margin financial statement, like the one just presented.)

So, what would happen if your master budget projections don't come true?

Well, let's find out. That is what Flexible Budgeting is for!

Look at the Contribution Margin Statement example again. To the right of the master budget, we have two Flexible Budget scenarios: The first flex's sales at 90% of the master. The second flex's sales at 110% of the master. Look at the variable expenses as a dollar amount - they change. However, notice the ratio (percentages) to sales? They are exactly the same for both scenarios. That is the nature of variable expenses. While changing sales levels, variable expenses have no additional impact on profitability. Contribution margin stays exactly the same.

Now, look at the fixed expenses of both the 90% and 110% flex scenarios. Here the dollar amounts do not change because they are fixed. But, the percent of sales amounts change due to the decrease and increase in sales. You can see that in the 90% flex scenario the fixed costs are higher as a percent, and all profitability has been eroded. Alternatively, in the 110% flex, a healthy profitability is reported. Again, this is economies of scale in action.

Although not shown in this writing, I often take flexible budgeting further. Planning and scenarios can be compared with balance sheet projections. Cash flow, inventory and debt levels can be figured in advance, for example.

The break even in all three scenarios, the master budget, the 90% flex, and the 110% flex are identical. Profit, of course, is the major difference.

The BIG lesson here is... Stop guessing! Take surprise out of the equation. Study the variable and fixed nature of your operational costs and plan for various scenarios. This will maximize your chances of success and allow your operation to grow more profitably.

29. CREATE A PERFORMANCE SCORECARD

The "Balanced Scorecard" & 4 Critical Success Factors that drive performance

Answer this question and write down your answer: Specifically, where do you want your business to be one year from now?

Congratulations for answering! You have taken the first step on the path to getting there. I will now show you the next steps to take towards achieving your goal.

A key to achieving any goal is having a plan that includes measurable performance actions. Such a plan is your annual financial budget. Your measurements lie in your performance reporting or your scorecard. This article is about how to use a performance scorecard as an organizational tool.

What is a Scorecard?

Scorecards are tools and techniques used to measure progress made toward achieving your goals. Those business people that do it properly have a significantly better chance of succeeding in their marketplace. Those that do not have usable reporting mechanisms generally rely more on chance. Simply put, performance reporting and scorecards improve your odds of success.

The "Balanced Scorecard" was introduced by Drs. Robert Kaplan and David Norton to readers of the Harvard Business Review in the 1990s. The objective of their scorecard is to assist companies in achieving strategic objectives using both financial and non-financial measurements. In its design, the "Balanced Scorecard" identifies four Critical Success Factors (CSF's) that drive performance: Financial, Customer, Internal Business Processes, and Learning and Growth. For each of these four performance factors, strategic objectives, measurements, targets, and initiatives are assigned.

Create a Performance Scorecard

There is no one size fits all. Your goals will be different from your peers even though you share the same industry and perhaps even the same market. You should consider your own strengths, weaknesses, opportunities, threats (SWOT). Be realistic. If you are weak in one area of your business, such as business processes, and strong in another area, such as customer service, realize this when designing your performance scorecard.

The following is an example of the process for creating a scorecard:

Overall Goal: This goes back to my initial question: "Where do you want to be one year from now?" Common answers to this question are often tied to sales or cash flow objectives. For this example let's say that the overall goal is: To increase cash flow by 100% (double cash on hand while holding liabilities constant).

Financial Measures: This is where you can define the hard numbers that you wish to track. Seeing how the overall goal is to increase cash flow, we need to document the specific objectives and measures that will affect the goal. For this example, we will use these strategic objectives: 10% revenue growth, 20% inventory to sales, 1:1 quick ratio. The associated measurements should be closely tracked on a monthly basis using your financial statements. If you wait to report on progress longer than a month, you may be too late to affect the desired result.

Customer Measures: To drive future performance, non-financial measures must be defined. Customer measures are the first. Common strategic objectives in this category are improvements in customer acquisition, customer retention, customer satisfaction, quality, and timeliness.

Customer acquisition involves increasing the base of new customers. Retention is keeping existing customers coming back. Both objectives are key to short and long term growth. Improving satisfaction, product quality, and service is an initiative that sets the organization apart from competitors. Timeliness has the dual goal of delivering product quickly while speeding up the revenue cycle.

Setting up systems that track and improve these customer related measures would result in happier customers, increased traffic, and better close rates. This would lead to greater sales volume. Then, the overall goal of increasing cash flow would be impacted.

Internal Business Process Measures: Financial and Customer critical success factors get the most attention from most independent businesses. The next two CSFs, Internal Business Process and Learning and Growth hold great opportunity as these factors could be better embraced by many managers.

The purpose of developing strong internal business processes is to achieve the best results. Well defined policies and procedures allow people to operate at higher capacities. This success factor is a primary reason why businesses of the same sales volume can be at opposite ends of the spectrum on measures of cash flow and profitability. For the purpose of my example, business processes that form the strategic objectives are: improving inventory control, increasing vendor performance, managing inventory better, becoming more customer-driven, and implementing a more effective Customer Relationship Management (CRM) system.

Internal business processes are necessary if you want to get positive momentum in your financial and customer measures. I suggest using a SWOT (Strengths/Weaknesses/Opportunities/Threats) analysis. It can help you flesh out ideas to improve in areas that you are lagging. Then you can decide which business constraints you want to try to address first and which innovations you wish to embrace.

Learning and Growth Measures: The final critical success factor in this performance scorecard is learning and growth. You might have the greatest plan and the best IT system in the world but without a well-trained and motivated team, goals are just dreams.

To accomplish any of your objectives, you must look to internal and external resources for help. You must have leaders within your organization that will step up and champion a project if you give them the chance. You should also look to industry experts to act as catalysts for direction and training with respect to learning and growth. There are no successful organizations that have "gotten there" on their own.

On a monthly and quarterly basis, assess your measures and adjust your strategy if necessary. Keep it dynamic. Add and delete items as necessary. Just be sure to always consider your critical success factors and the important role they play in your business.

Think of your scorecard as a master performance report with other reports providing supporting information. This will help you focus on your primary goal. Using a Scorecard will give you a greater chance of success.

The Performance Scorecard Basic Example:

Balance Scorecard, for Year 20XX				
Primary Overall Goal: To increase cash flow by 100%				
	Strategic Objective	**Supporting Initiatives / Measurements**	**Targets**	**Result - Q1**
Financial Measures	Change in cash flow: 100%	Track monthly on Financial Statements	100% increase by May 31	15%
	10% Revenue growth	Financial Statements for delivered and Sales performance for written business	8% over last year by Aug	5%
	Reduce inventory to sales ratio to 20%	Financial Statements	22% by Sept	24%
	Achieve a quick ratio of 1:1	Financial Statements	.9 by Sept	0.85
Customer Measures	Customer Acquisition	New traffic count	1000 new customer visits per month	150 new visits
	Customer Retention	Repeat business ratio	20%	25%
	Customer Satisfaction	Returns, complaints, surveys	Goal of 99% satisfaction rating by YE	94%
	Quality of Product and Service	Service issues by vendor and reason	Fewer than 20 unresolved issues at any one time	18
	Timeliness	Time from order to delivery	Average for special order - under 5 weeks	7 weeks average lead time
Internal Business Processes	Inventory Control improvement	Routine cycle inventories with bar coding	99% inventory accuracy by Sept	85%
	Vendor Performance enhancement	Track GMROI of top 10 vendors by volume	Achieve a GMROI of minimum of $2.5 for top vendors by Year end	$2.25
	Manage inventory better	5 SMART Steps; spot winners, maintain a proper inventory mix, auto ID dogs, Reward performance, target market customers	Implement with Consultant in July	scheduled
	Become more customer focused	CRM systems	Implement with consultant in July	pending
Learning and Growth	Motivate employees better	Establish Pay for Performance program	1 new incentive program for each department by Aug	n/a
	Skill development in inventory flow operations	Onsite training by industry consultant	Consultant chosen and scheduled for week of July 18th	pending
	Benchmark against peers	Join a Peer performance group	Kaizen group by Aug	joined

30. TIPS FROM THE FIELD

Here is an interview that I participated in just prior to the publication of Field Tips.

What questions would you ask someone who has intimately worked with hundreds of businesses? We asked David McMahon. He has travelled the world for the past 15 years taking the role of a Consulting CFO and is a performance group leader. He analyzes productivity, determines strategy to improve and trains in the tactics to accomplish results. As you can imagine, this brings up some important questions. Here are some of his answers:

What do you think is the most important factor for success?

David McMahon:

"Attitude."

"I have seen companies in the same market area producing the same volume with totally different results. Take 2 businesses in the same town. Both had $5 million in sales on average for 3 years. One had huge cash flow, happy employees, and satisfied customers. The other had stressed out employees, upset customers and eventually went out of business after 25 years. The driving factor that set them apart was attitude."

How did attitude account for one succeeding and the other failing?

David McMahon:

"The attitude came from the top. The owner CEO believed in a culture of continuous improvement. He was one of the smartest business people that I have encountered but he did not think that he was that smart. He continently sought to find new ways to innovate his business. He was willing to do things that his competition would not do. He constantly tried to get the upper hand on his competition. He surrounded himself with people that he respected who shared his goal for self-improvement.

The owner of the other operation thought he knew it all. He believed in the philosophy of, "if it ain't broken don't fix it."

Eventually a gap widened over time between these 2 businesses. One sunk more and more money into advertising and big sales to produce leads. The other focused on improving sales professionalism, inventory flow and customer service. You know who survived."

"There is ALWAYS something that can be improved"

OK, so for businesses that commit to continual improvement, where do you see the biggest opportunity?

David McMahon:

"I see that many businesses leave too many dollars on the table. For example, smart managers understand that gross margins are a state of mind. Unless you are selling a commodity and delivering the exact same product and service as your competition, there is price flexibility. Pricing should be based on value perception and filling the price points desired. Those that strictly use a cost mark-up

184

pricing approach, end up with odd ball pricing. They miss opportunity. You see prices ending in 44, 09, and 75. That is usually garbage pricing. All new pricing for items of over $200 retail should be end in $99, in my opinion. Do you think if someone wants something for $557 they would not pay $599? Or, what about if you see something at $809? That is not a price – come on - it is $799 or $899!

However, there are some retailers who make a case for oddball pricing – but that is longer consumer-psychological discussion.

Whatever the pricing strategy, you can't have gaps missing in price points. That is a big reason why customers walk.

Prices should be set based on value and make sense in your line-up."

How about sales? What do you see businesses doing to increase sales volume?

David McMahon:

"Well most business are not great businesses. Below average performers often just use the latest advertising gimmick to hopefully increase door swings. Then they close their same percent of leads. That is fine, but the great businesses are the ones who can increase sales when customer traffic remains constant. When these businesses experience an uptick in traffic they are humongously profitable. They do this by focusing on improving the selling process. They track traffic, selling opportunities, average sale, and close rates, amongst other metrics. They know their numbers, so they are able to set benchmarks for sales management. You can't manage sales on volume only. The factors that make up the volume are what matters.

The managers who "get it" are using CRM systems so they can improve the follow-up between the salesperson and their client. There is a much greater close rate per customer as opposed to "per traffic" using this approach. This is because they produce return visits or be-backs"

So there is not a silver bullet then to increasing sales?

David McMahon:

"The CRM system is a silver rocket launcher.

All I can say is that many stores need to get off the media cocaine somewhat. I once heard that advertising is like a tax that businesses pay on being unremarkable. I believe in investing some of that marketing spend into improving the selling process and servicing the customer more professionally."

Seeing that you are skeptical of media, what advertising have you seen that does work?

David McMahon:

"I am more skeptical of the general practices out there. There are some businesses that are very successful with media marketing. Do you want to know their secret?"

Of course!

David McMahon:

"Those that are successful are not afraid to fail! They try over and over again. They fail sometimes and they eventually succeed. They play a numbers game. They then become masters, get a formula and then succeed more often. Those that can pull traffic in from TV advertise over and over again on TV. They get good at it and build a market presence. They get penetration. Those that are good at internet advertise a lot on internet. Those that are good at circulars advertise a lot with circulars. Those that are good with direct mail advertise a lot with direct mail. Radio people are radio people. They all fail sometimes but they become very good in the media of their choice and they eventually pull in the traffic. They also get a better cost per ad due to their commitment.

Alternatively, those that look for a magic bullet and try something once in one media and then go to another media and try something else - never really penetrate the market and they pay more for nothing. They have not failed enough in one place to get really good and they have not built exposure. Also, if you are up against businesses that own the media channel or desired slot, unless you have some deep pockets, you may want to look at alternatives. Marketers need their niche.

My same theory applies to other things too. Do you want to be good at selecting new merchandise? Well, you better have good inventory management so you can buy as often as possible. Or, want to be great at selling a certain product? Well you better try and try and try until you get it."

Other than the top line, which other areas are people improving in?

David McMahon:

"There really are countless ways. It depends on the specific operation. People should seek to improve the area of their business that will have the greatest effect on profitability and be the easiest and least costly to do so. I'll give you a few examples outside of sales and gross margin:

First, Delivery – some companies are able to fully offset all their delivery and shipping expenses with delivery income. They figure out exactly what the delivery costs them as a percent of sales and then figure out a fee structure that will produce the income. The simplest way that I have seen is to charge a dollar amount up to a certain transaction level and then a percent of the transaction afterwards. I would even go so far as saying that if a salesperson needs to give a discount on delivery to make the sale, that's fine, but it comes out of their commission.

As well with respect to deliveries, many are starting to streamline routing and the paperwork process by using mobile products and apps that are available.

Warehousing – Everyone should have 99.9% inventory accuracy. Bar coding is the only way to accomplish this. The realization of this is getting to be universal. I think if you have over $1 Million in annual volume or $300,000 in inventory, at cost, you should make the investment. It pays off easily and quickly. Smart operators invest money to protect their assets.

Purchasing Inventory – this is an area even business veterans continue to struggle with. It requires constant attention. If you carry too little, your selection thins out and there is less to show customers. If you carry too much, your cash flow suffers. Many see inventory as a double edge sword. But it does not have to be!

Take emotion out of the equation. Intimately know the GMROI of your overall business each month. Track GMROI by Category. Track GMROI by Vendor. Then track GMROI by categories within vendor and vendors within categories. This will show you where to buy and where to hold or drop. It's like the Kenny Rogers song, "The Gambler" – you got to know when to hold-em and know when to fold-em.

Acting on solid analysis helps you create a better mix. For businesses that are over inventoried – they should have a buying freeze on new merchandise and still buy top margin producing items.

And don't be afraid to discount FAST on merchandise that does not sell. It is a SUNK cost. That means that the money has been spent and the cost should not really be considered. The non-selling merchandise costs you more in lost valuable floor space. Would you return it to your vendor for cost, if they would pay you back? I never heard anyone answer no to this question. What's the difference?

Profitability – many businesses are so top line focused that their vision is clouded from the bottom-line. They need to have one eye on the top line and the other eye on the bottom line. Acceptable standards should be set for operating in all cost categories. A business structure needs to be in place that delivers at least a 5% bottom line during a bad sales month. Anything less than this over time causes liquidity issues. The businesses in the CEO performance groups that I lead strive for double digit bottom lines. That means 10% of Sales in Net Income. Great performing retailers are getting this month in, month out."

Are there any areas of peoples' businesses that they have trouble improving in?

David McMahon:

"There are a lot of independent businesses that have questionable financial reporting. I find this concerning because the ultimate management report are the Financial Statements. They tell the executive management team the scorecard each month. They are the basis for future improvement. Without accurate or timely information, businesses lose focus and run off the seat of their pants. They become reactive rather than proactive –fighting fires as they come up.

It is the CEO's or Owner's job to ensure the best business decisions are being made. If their business is not large enough to afford an experienced Certified Accountant or MBA as Professional CFO then they should contract with a Consulting CFO that works on a part time basis to provide them with the required financial counsel. A qualified CFO is a CEO's right hand advisor."

So where would you advise a business to start improving?

David McMahon:

"I believe a business needs to start with looking at their master management reports: That is their balance sheet, profit and loss statement, and statement of cash flow. Then, they need to figure their break even and compare their performance indicators with standards. From there opportunities show there selves. If the opportunity is Gross Margin, set a strategy and focus tactics on that. If the opportunity is underperforming sales, set a strategy and focus tactics on that. If the opportunity is purchasing practices and merchandise management, set a strategy and focus tactics on that. Track the results – eventually the improvements will show on the bottom line and in your bank!"

APPENDIX A: METRICS & KPI'S

Here is a quick reference guide to a selection of key performance indicators (KPI's) and metrics. The important thing with metrics is knowing how to track them and how to improve them, without harming another area of the operation. If you want to improve something, you must start by tracking it. Then you can strategize and execute specific tactics. In this list I am not going to suggest what number you should strive to be at. That ultimately depends on your goals and standards for your unique situation. I hope that you find this list useful and I hope you enjoyed my writings in Field Tips. Cheers! ~ David

Liquidity, Solvency, Debt Ratios

KPI	Formula	Definition or Use
Current Ratio	Current Assets / Current Liabilities	Ability to pay for short term debt with short term assets.
Quick Ratio	(Current Assets - Inventory) / Current Liabilities	Ability to pay for short term debt with liquid assets (Cash, AR).
Cash Ratio	Cash / Current Liabilities	Ability to pay for short term debt with cash.
Change in Cash	(Current Cash Book Balance - Prior Period Balance) / Prior Period Balance	To track if your actions are increasing cash position. Cash is King.
Working Capital	Current Assets - Current Liabilities	Solvency measure. A negative number is insolvent.
Debt to Equity	Total liabilities / shareholder equity	The proportion of debt and equity used to finance assets.
Accounts Payable (AP) Turnover	Total Supplier Purchases / Average AP Balance	Liquidity measure to track the rate you pay off suppliers.
Days Purchases in AP	365 / AP Turns	Average number of days AP is held.
Accounts Payable to Inventory	(AP / Inventory) x 100	The percentage of outstanding AP to inventory.

Operating Activity Ratios

KPI	Formula	Definition or Use
Accounts Receivable (AR) Turns	Credit Sales / Average AR	Average number of times AR collected during the year.
Days Sales in AR	365 / AR Turns	Average collection period in days.
Inventory Turns	Cost of Goods Sold / Average Inventory	Number of times inventory is sold during a year.
Days Sales in Inventory	365 / Inventory Turns	Number of days to sell average inventory.
Operating Cycle for Cash	Days sales in AR + Days sales in inventory	How quickly you will receive cash once inventory is acquired or manufactured. A shorter operating cycle turns into increased cash flow.

Revenue Analysis Ratios

KPI	Formula	Definition or Use
Sales	Average Sale x Close Rate x # of Selling Opportunities	"Top Line". Tracking the parts of the sales equation through a CRM system allows you to gain the knowledge needed to effect it.
Close Rate	# of Sales / # of Selling Opportunities	Effectiveness in converting leads to sales.
Revenue per Opportunity	Sales / # of Selling Opportunities	The value in sales dollars of each customer lead.
Sales to Plan	(Targeted Sales / Actual Sales) x 100	The percent of actual sales to sales goal. Want to be above 100%. Under 100% results in less profit and cash than expected.
Sales Growth	(Current period sales - last period sales)/last period sales) x 100	Measure effectiveness and trends.
Same Store Sales % (SSS, comparable sales)	Compare sales growth of 2 periods after excluding sales produced from new revenue centers.	For chain operations to determine what part of new sales is from growth and what part is from adding new revenue outlets.
Sales per square foot	Sales / total square foot selling space	Highlights the value of floor space. A measure of efficiency in using display.
Sales per Selling Employee	Sales / total # of selling employees	Gauge the effectiveness and capacity of sales force.
% of Repeat Customers	# of returning customers / total number of customer opportunities	A customer service and CRM measure.
Sales per Opportunity per Salesperson per Month	Sales / selling opportunity / # of salespeople / 12	To gauge the effectiveness and capacity of a sales force. If there are more opportunities than a sales force can handle properly, customer experience suffers.

Profitability Analysis

KPI	Formula	Definition or Use
Gross Margin % (GM) (gross profit margin)	(Sales – Cost of Goods Sold) / Sales	The percent of sales that you have left over to pay for all your operating costs and make a profit.
Administrative Cost %	General admin costs / sales	Benchmarking, budgeting, goal setting.
Occupancy Cost %	Occupancy costs / sales	Benchmarking, budgeting, goal setting.
Advertising Cost %	Media and Marketing costs / sales	Benchmarking, budgeting, goal setting.
Selling Cost %	Selling and commission costs / sales	Benchmarking, budgeting, goal setting.
Vendor Service Credit %	Vendor credits / Sales	Measure effectiveness of obtaining vendor chargeback's.
Net Delivery / Shipping %	(Delivery Expense - Income) / Sales	Benchmarking, budgeting, goal setting.
Warehousing Cost %	Distribution Center Costs / Sales	Benchmarking, budgeting, goal setting.
Total Operating Cost %	All net operating costs / Sales	A measure of total operating cost efficiency.
Finance Cost %	Financing Costs and Bank Charges / Sales	Benchmarking, budgeting, goal setting.
Net Income % (Net profit Margin)	(Sales - COGS - All other expenses) / Sales	"Bottom Line". To measure profitability. The $ that adds to or takes away from cash flow.

Break Even Analysis

KPI	Formula	Definition or Use
Variable Expense %	Variable costs (costs that are incurred with sales) / Sales	To understand cost mix. To figure break-even. The costs that move in proportion with sales as a percent. As a dollar amount, they go up when sales go up.
Fixed Expense %	Fixed costs (costs that are incurred regardless of revenue amount) / Sales	The costs that stay the same as a dollar amount, when sales fluctuate. As a percent they go down as sales go up.
Contribution Margin	(Sales - Variable Expense) / Sales	The % of sales that contributes to profit after the break-even sales are reached.
Break-even Sales	Fixed Costs / Contribution Margin	The sales level that must be surpassed to make a profit.
Sales to Reach Desired Profitability	(Desired Profitability + Fixed Cost) / Contribution Margin %	To help set sales goals that translate into profits and cash flow.

Inventory and Purchasing Analysis Ratios

KPI	Formula	Definition or Use
GMROI (Gross Margin Return on Inventory Investment)	GM $ annualized or projected / Average Inventory	The ultimate inventory management metric for overall business, category and vendor. Improvement directly translates into profit and cash.
Inventory to Sales	Average Inventory / Annualized or projected Sales	To determine target inventory level for a sales volume. Open to buy consideration. Helps keep cash flow constant.
Available Merchandise Not on Display %	# of SKU's available for sale that are not shown / # of SKU's	To ensure your customers and salespeople can see all the product that you stock. A merchandising efficiency measure.
% of Merchandise that can be delivered or shipped, not scheduled	# of sales invoices in stock and not scheduled to be delivered / # sales invoices in stock	To help deliver as fast as possible to generate higher turns. Measure of delivery and shipping efficiency.
Best Seller In Stock Days %	Best Selling Items In stock Days / Best Selling Items Total Days	To improve the time best selling merchandise is shown. Increases sales. Measure of purchasing and merchandising effectiveness.
% of Inventory aged under 60 days	Inventory aged under 60 days / Total inventory value	Shows the mix of inventory. A higher % shows a greater amount of newer inventory and general a faster turning floor. Merchandising and purchasing effectiveness.

Capital Structure Ratios (Long term debt evaluation)

KPI	Formula	Definition or Use
Financial Leverage	Total Assets / Total Equity	Measure of how much the business is financed with debt. A 2 means liabilities are = to equity. Has a magnifying effect on earnings and loss due to the fixed cost of debt.
Debt to Total Assets	Total Debt / Total Assets	Proportion of assets financed with debt. Lower is better for creditors.
Debt to Equity	Total Debt / Total Equity	Shows ability to pay for long term debt. Reliance on debt.
Long-term Debt to Equity	(Total Debt - Current Liabilities) / Equity	Compare only long-term debt financing.
Interest Coverage (Times Interest Earned)	Earnings Before Interest & Taxes (EBIT) / Interest Expense	Ability to pay interest on debt through regular operations.

APPENDIX B: REPORTING & SYSTEMS SUGGESTIONS

Here is a quick reference guide to some reports and IT (information technology) processes. Depending on what systems you are running, reports will go by slightly different names. You should be able to get this and other information that you require for decision making – provided you are feeding your ERP (enterprise resource planning) system with data properly. Again, I hope that you find this list useful and I hope you enjoyed my writings in Field Tips. Cheers! ~ David

Daily

- Written Sales – to review sales numbers, to look for additional customer follow-up, to verify accuracy.
- Cash Report – to balance cash and match with bank deposits.
- Customer Traffic Counts – to measure flow of customer visits. Use automated door counters.
- Selling Opportunities – to track customers served and to determine close rate.
- Daily Follow up List – to allow sales and service employees to be proactive with customer's needs.
- Special Order PO's – to get custom orders processed with vendors, fast.
- Stock PO's – to order best sellers and new merchandise when needed.
- PO Acknowledgements – to verify that the supplier is processing the PO's properly, update costs, enter estimated shipping dates so customers and salespeople have information.
- Bar code labels – to prepare in advance for the next day's merchandise receiving.
- Merchandise Receiving Reports – to get stock merchandise into inventory and on display ASAP, to get customer merchandise scheduled for delivery or pick up ASAP.
- Merchandise Transfers – to organize location transfers and keep inventory locations accurate and timely.

- Picking Lists / Packing Lists – to prepare outgoing merchandise for customers.
- Delivery/Shipping Receipts and Routing – to efficiently organize outgoing orders.
- Work Orders – to schedule and track service jobs.
- Accounts Payable – enter merchandise and freight invoices after merchandise is received. Verify inventory costing. Enter expense invoices as they are received so debt to vendors is known.

Weekly

- Salesperson Goals – month to date. To track progress on written sales vs plan.
- Salesperson Open Tasks – to manage customer follow-up.
- Open Quotes – to follow up with customers with pending sales.
- Merchandise to Display – to display merchandise that is not on showroom floors yet in a warehouse.
- Sales Orders Ready for Delivery, Pick up, or Shipping. To notify and schedule customers, fast.
- Bank reconciliation – to keep current with cash reconciliation between bank and books. Do this daily or weekly to find issues faster and speed up month end reporting.
- Best Seller Purchase Reorders – to avoid best seller stock outs. Maximize sales.
- Accounts Payable – for payment processing.
- Commissions and Payroll processing. (can be semi-monthly, bi-weekly, monthly)
- AR Invoicing and Statements – for collections on customers owing.
- Open to buy – to keep track of inventory to sales level and determine if new purchases are required.
- Inventory "Nail-down" Item Review – To keep best sellers on display. Maximize sales.
- Past Due Purchase Orders – for order follow-up with vendors.
- Damaged Reports – to take faster action on issues with unsaleable inventory.

- Customer Service Issues – to be proactive with customer service issues.
- Best Seller Lists – to keep up with the latest hot items.

Monthly / Quarterly / Annual

- Financial Statements – to review the master management reports. Balance Sheet, Profit and Loss, Statement of Cash Flow.
- Sales Tax and other compliance reporting.
- Salesperson Results – written and delivered sales. Track average sale, close rate, return customer rate, revenue per up, number of leads, gross margin.
- Customer Traffic and Opportunity Analysis.
- Sales Performance Analysis by Vendor – Track volume, GMROI, GM, Turns, % of Total Sales.
- Sales Performance Analysis by Category – Track volume, GMROI, GM, Turns, % of Total Sales.
- Sales Performance Analysis by Vendor within Category
- Sales Performance Analysis by Category within Vendor
- Sales Performance Analysis ranked by top selling items
- Inventory Markdowns – to identify and take action on stagnant merchandise (Dogs).
- Line-up reporting – to determine # of slots in various product price points.
- E-newsletters – to build a customer following.
- AR Aging – financial reconciliation.
- AP Aging – financial reconciliation.
- Open PO aging – to see incoming inventory for cash flow consideration.
- Conduct 1 on 1 meetings with employees.
- Scorecards – update performance reports and actions with respect to goals.
- Budgets, Projections, Pro Formas – To forecast profits & cash flow. To update financial targets and adjust strategy to changing business conditions.

David W. McMahon, CMA

APPENDIX C: RETAIL EFFICIENCY RANKING

Efficient businesses with effective leaders and employees have the greatest earnings year after year. In tough times, they are able to produce stable cash flow. In times of growth, they have huge earnings.

Here is an informal and non-scientific ranking that you can use to help gauge where your company is performing well and where it can use some operational improvements.

	1 point Disagree	2 points We are average	3 points YES!
Our inventory is 99% accurate. Anyone can locate inventory fast.			
Our salespeople can independently answer our customers questions regarding inventory, order status, and account status.			
All conversation notes between our employees and customers are entered electronically.			
Sales are entered in front of our customers as the transaction occurs. Receipts are emailed.			
We follow-up with thank you emails and calls.			
We know our in-store and on-line traffic.			
We track leads for the customers who visit and do not buy yet.			
We follow-up with potential customers by scheduling tasks in our IT system.			
Our sales manager knows average sale, close ratio, number of opportunities, and revenue per up. She/he executes tactics to improve the metrics.			
Our sales manager is effective in finding, training, and developing salespeople.			
Our cash is balanced every day in less than 20 minutes.			
We use our customer database to make the best use of our advertising dollars. We target market customers.			
Receiving is processed immediately.			
We use bar coding for inventory tracking.			
We track all customer service issues in our system and have a vendor charge back (VCB) system.			
We track GMROI and have a clear strategy to increase it.			
We carry the proper amount of inventory to sales, so that cash flow is maximized.			

198

We systematically identify slow merchandise and take actions to turn our dogs into cash.			
99% of our available merchandise is displayed.			
Over 90% of complete sales are scheduled for delivery. Very few deliveries have issues.			
Billing of customers is timely and accounts receivable is correct and controllable.			
Our best sellers are tracked, identified, and displayed.			
We use an efficient system to reorder best sellers so we are stocked at the right level.			
Distribution management and warehousing is lean and effective for our sales volume.			
We conduct weekly operations meetings and set action items. We also conduct 1 on 1 monthly employee feedback meetings.			
We have pay-for-performance programs for most employees. It motivate them to reach their goals.			
Our financials are on time (no later than the 10th of the next month) each month. We completely understand them.			
We always have enough cash to make payroll, keep all of our payables current. We have a strong quick ratio.			
We completely reconcile our bank accounts in a timely fashion.			
We reconcile our sub ledgers to the general ledger and verify balances on the balance sheet. This helps ensure financial and margin accuracy.			
We have proven that we can execute our plan and strategy.			
We have a clear digital marketing strategy.			
We innovate.			
Totals			

Total all columns for your score. If you need improvement, that is ok! Most of the best retailers today had to make significant organizational enhancements to get where they are now.

0 – 50	(F) Failing grade. Immediately get help. If you continue at this performance level, you will need to take loans to pay for the inefficiencies.
50 – 60	(D) Barely passing. The management team should put together an action plan to focus on underlying performance issues.
61 – 70	(C) You are average. You are on the cusp of going either way: success or failure.
71 – 80	(B) You are a decent operator. You definitely have implemented some best practices. Learn from what is working and why, then apply that attitude to your weaknesses.
81 – 90	(A) You are almost there. A few slight changes and you can become a best-of-breed company. You are doing so many things right. Keep on improving!
90 – 99	(A+) You have a model operation. You are a credit to your industry, a fantastic place to work and shop!

David W. McMahon, CMA

SPECIAL OFFER

Complementary Business Analysis:

- Assess financial accuracy.
- Liquidity & cash flow review.
- Operating activity analysis.
- Revenue analysis.
- Provide an opinion based on the Balance Sheet, P&L, Cash flow Statement.
- Break even analysis.
- Recommendations to improve profitability and cash flow.

***Subject to scheduling. Scheduling allows for 1 or 2 complimentary business analysis projects per month.

***Just email to McMahonLIVE@gmail.com and reference this offer.

Ordering Additional Copies

http://tinyurl.com/fieldtipsbook

http://tinyurl.com/fieldtips

ABOUT THE AUTHOR

David W. McMahon is an organizational improvement specialist. He has helped increase the cash flow & profitability in hundreds of companies. As a CMA (Certified Management Accountant), he focuses on the execution of strategy in business. In his leisure time, he trains for Triathlons and is an Ironman Podium finisher. David lives with his beautiful family – Raja, Chase, & Vela – in San Diego, CA. Feel free to contact David for speaking and consulting engagements.

McMahonLIVE@gmail.com .